MILKWEED BUTTERFLIES

MILKWEED

Monarchs,

Illustrations by the author

Author of "Exploring the World
of Social Insects," etc.

With a Foreword by John Pallister,
Department of Entomology,
American Museum of
Natural History

Hilda Simon

BUTTERFLIES
Models, and Mimics

NEW YORK
THE VANGUARD PRESS

Text and illustrations
Copyright © 1969 by Hilda Simon

Published simultaneously in Canada by the
Copp Clark Publishing Company, Ltd., Toronto

All rights reserved. No part of this publication may
be reproduced or transmitted in any form or by any means,
electronic or mechanical, including photocopy, recording,
or any information storage or retrieval system, or otherwise,
without the written permission of the publisher, except
by a reviewer who may wish to quote brief passages and
up to three illustrations in connection with a review for a
newspaper, magazine, radio, or television.
Manufactured in the United States of America

Library of Congress Card Catalogue Number: 68-56601
Standard Book Number: 8149-0006-2

To all those who rejoice when they see a butterfly on a summer day, and who want to help protect these beautiful creatures' place in the sun.

Contents

Foreword	11
Introduction	15
Milkweed Butterflies of the Tropics	25
The Wonders of Mimicry	41
Introducing the Monarch	55
The Caterpillar	63
The Chrysalis	71
Summer Life	79
Migration	87
Raising Monarchs at Home	101
Appendix	109
Diagrams	110
Glossary of Zoological Terms	114
Index	117

List of Illustrations

Three different species of milkweed butterflies	Title page
Butterflies in a meadow	14-15
Various species of Blues	16-17
Moth, skipper, and swallowtail butterfly	18
Upper and lower wing surfaces of a Morpho butterfly	20
Enlarged scales and scale structures of a Morpho	21
Enlarged portion of a butterfly wing	22
Butterfly scales, greatly enlarged	23
Three tropical Danaids, or milkweed butterflies	26-27
Six different species of Old-World milkweed butterflies	30-31
Subspecies of the African monarch	32
Caterpillar of the African monarch	33
Indo-Australian milkweed butterfly	35
A species of Euploea, a tropical Danaid	36
Wing and body proportions in two different Danaids	37
Six New-World species of milkweed butterflies	38-39
Two Danaid "models" (center) and two mimics (right and left)	42-43
A common stick insect	44
A hornet "model" and its moth "mimic"	46
A beetle "model" and its moth "mimic"	47
Central-American Danaid "model"	48
Central-American nymphalid "mimic"	49
The African monarch (center) and two mimics. The nonmimetic males are shown on the right.	52-53
Monarchs on a flower	57
Map showing distribution of North American monarch	59
The viceroy, a "mimic" of the monarch	60
The queen, a North American Danaid	61
Monarch caterpillars on milkweed	64-65
Monarch eggs, greatly enlarged	66
Newly hatched (left) and very young monarch caterpillars	67
Monarch caterpillars in various growth stages	69
Two monarch chrysalids on butterfly weed	72-73

Monarch caterpillar ready for pupating	74
Monarch caterpillar sheds its last skin	75
Monarch chrysalis shortly before emergence of butterfly	76
Monarch, moments after having emerged from pupal shell	77
Monarch and other butterflies in a summer meadow	81
A common species of praying mantis	82
Monarch on a flower	83
Male and female monarch during mating flight	85
Migrating monarchs	88-89
Map showing the migrations of the European painted lady butterfly	91
Monarchs gathering in groups for migration	92
Monarchs in their winter quarters	95
Female monarch laying eggs on milkweed	97
Map showing the routes followed by migrating monarchs	98-99
Monarch chrysalis and newly-emerged butterfly raised in a home	103
A common North American species of milkweed	105
Flying monarch	107

DIAGRAMS:

Ancestral tree of insects	110
Various forms of development among insects	111
The parts of a butterfly	112
Wing veins in two different species of butterflies	112
Parts of a caterpillar	113
Internal parts of a caterpillar	113
Transverse cut through a caterpillar's body	113

Foreword

Here is another book by Miss Hilda Simon, the talented and charming writer of books about the natural sciences and insects. Not only does Miss Simon write the books; she illustrates them as well with superb and accurate drawings in color.

Milkweed Butterflies: Monarchs, Models, and Mimics has an introduction on butterflies in general that gives the reader a closer knowledge of the life of these beautiful and interesting insects. Some of the milkweed butterflies of the tropics are illustrated and described.

Then Miss Simon takes up the complex subject of mimicry, a theory propounded about one hundred years ago by the famous naturalists and scientists Bates, Müller, Wallace, and Darwin. Both in text and drawings Miss Simon discusses the principles of mimicry in simple language easily understood by young readers. I am certain that if Bates, Wallace, and the other early scientists were alive today, they would agree with me that the subject has been handled with great clarity and understanding.

The fascinating life of our monarch butterfly is told so well that we will all want to go out-of-doors to see the monarchs at home. To see a monarch slowly gliding, so lazily and unafraid, on outspread wings over a field, is one of the most delightful sights of a summer day. The monarch is one of the few butterflies that has this remarkable flight.

What a drab world this would be without the monarch, its relatives, and all the other butterflies to brighten the landscape with their color. We must do more to protect them. I am sure Miss Simon's book will be of great service in bringing to the layman something of the value butterflies contribute to our life.

JOHN C. PALLISTER
Research Associate, Department of Entomology
The American Museum of Natural History

INTRODUCTION

Introduction

Butterflies! The very word evokes visions of bright color, beauty, and gaiety. Pictures of carefree childhood or lazy vacation days, sun-drenched meadows, blue skies, and sweet-smelling breezes, with flowering gardens in full bloom, flash through the mind when we think of butterfly wings in the sunlight.

Although most other insects may be feared or disliked — often unjustly — most persons rarely think of butterflies as insects, and they are an exception to this rule. Rare, indeed, is the person who does not enjoy watching the colorful, delicate creatures flitting from flower to flower in their search for sweet nectar. The garden-loving English

people are ardent butterfly enthusiasts and consider no flower bed quite complete without them. Sir Winston Churchill once ordered a large number of live butterflies from a dealer and had them released on his grounds to enhance one of his garden parties. Even the British Parliament has concerned itself with butterflies: money appropriations for measures designed to halt the alarming decrease in the butterfly population — a phenomenon unfortunately occurring today in all civilized countries — have been considered by the House of Commons.

Anyone who becomes interested in butterflies, regardless of the degree of seriousness, does well to acquaint himself with some of the basic facts that apply to the entire group. Despite great variation among the different families and even species, basic features of development and body structure are shared by all.* For anyone who has familiarized himself with these features the study of a group, or even a single species, will be easier and much more rewarding.

Two groups, the moths and the butterflies, make up the huge order of *Lepidoptera*, or scale-winged insects. The moths are the larger, the more primitive, and generally the less attractive of the two. Despite the existence of many species of large and beautiful moths, the majority are rather small, drab-looking insects colored predomi-

*A table of zoological classification appears in the appendix, which also contains diagrams of insect anatomy and development.

nantly in grays and browns. Butterflies, on the other hand, are most often at least medium-sized, usually handsome, and, in many cases, with wings that are strikingly patterned and colored.

Because they are *advanced* insects, all moths and butterflies go through the same complex *metamorphosis,* a complete change of body form. This metamorphosis consists of four stages — egg, larva, pupa, and winged adult. In many other advanced insects, however, the results are neither as spectacular nor as beautiful as those that produce a butterfly. Scarcely anyone would claim, for instance, that the metamorphosis of a white grub into a black, winged fly can compare to the miracle that transforms a rather ugly caterpillar into a delicate, often exquisitely colored and patterned creature. This transformation is especially gratifying when we remember that butterflies neither bite nor sting, nor do they transmit germs. On the contrary, the adults are helpful as pollinators of our flowers and fruit-tree blossoms. All these factors permit us to enjoy their beauty without reservation, and to protect them where we can. Even though caterpillars of certain species do some harm because they feed on cultivated plants, very few of our native butterflies are among them. Many moth caterpillars, on the other hand, are numbered among our most serious agricultural pests.

As mentioned earlier, all butterflies have the same basic development and body structure. After passing through the first three stages — egg, caterpillar, and pupa, all of which will be described in detail in later chapters — the adult insect emerges ready and well equipped for its airborne, nectar-seeking existence. As in all insects, the body consists of three parts: head, thorax, and abdomen. The thorax bears a pair of legs on each of its three segments. In several butterfly families, including the milkweed butterflies with which this book deals,

Moth (left) and butterfly (right) represent the two large groups that make up the order of Lepidoptera. The skipper (center) belongs to a group of primitive butterflies considered to be closely related to the moths.

the first pair of legs is so foreshortened that it is almost invisible. These butterflies, therefore, are functionally four-legged and use their short front legs only as brushes for cleaning their feelers.

The feelers, or *antennae*, are the most eye-catching feature of the butterfly's head. In contrast to those of moths, the feelers end in little clubs, or knobs. Serving as the insect's nose, they guide it to sweet-smelling flowers. The butterfly has two large compound eyes, like those of bees, flies, and many other insects. These eyes are made up of thousands of individual organs of sight joined together. Beneath its head, and neatly coiled up like a watchspring when not in use, the butterfly carries its sucking tube, or *proboscis*, popularly called the tongue. This sucking tube consists of two parts that fit into each other. With it, the insect can reach deep into the throats of flowers to suck their nectar.

One of the most interesting features of the butterfly's body resides in the soles of its feet, which are equipped with extremely sensitive taste organs. Tasting food with the feet may seem peculiar to us, but

Introduction

it is very practical for the butterfly. Because parts of a flower are covered with sweet secretions, the insect has only to touch the blossom with its feet to determine whether a good source of nectar has been found. If the test proves positive, the long sucking tube is automatically uncoiled and thrust into the heart of the blossom. If the test proves negative, the butterfly goes on to the next flower without wasting time. Experiments with monarchs have shown these taste organs may be as much as twenty-five hundred times more sensitive to sweet substances than is the human tongue. Translated into practical terms, this means that such butterflies could detect traces of sugar in solutions that would have to be twenty-five hundred times as strong to taste even slightly sweet to us!

The butterfly's abdomen, as well as the thorax, is frequently covered with fine furlike hairs. It usually consists of nine segments. Breathing pores, or *spiracles,* are located on both sides of the abdomen and thorax. In some cases, the furlike covering of the body is so dense that the segments as well as the breathing holes are difficult to spot unless the insect is examined closely with a magnifying glass.

The butterfly's most distinctive feature, of course, is its wings. They are large and, like those of bees, flies, and many other insects, consist of a glassy, transparent *membrane,* a kind of thin, parchment-like skin. This membrane is supported and stiffened by a network of hollow ribs, or veins, somewhat in the way the sailcloth wings of early airplanes were stiffened by wood or metal frames. Both the arrangement and the number of these veins differ in the various groups, and thus serve as a means of identification and classification for the naturalist.

The wings of most butterflies, unlike those of insects such as bees, wasps, and flies, have beautiful colors and patterns, owing to the thousands and thousands of tiny scales that cover both the upper and under sides of the wings. These scales are loosely attached, come off when the wing is touched, and then look like little bits of colored dust. Considering the minute size of the scales, and the tremendous number needed to

Upper wing surfaces of a Morpho butterfly. The blue color is not created by pigment. It is a structural color resulting from light refraction.

The underwing surfaces of the same Morpho show entirely different colors and patterns. These brown hues are pigment colors.

cover just one wing, it is truly amazing to find wing patterns so varied, so intricate, and yet so uniformly repeated in each individual of a species.

The colors we see on a butterfly's wings may be either *pigmental* or *structural* in origin. The pigmented scales get their color from actual coloring matter, or pigments, such as we use in dyes, inks, and paints. The structural colors, on the other hand, owe their existence, not to chemicals, but to the very special, minute structures of the scale sur-

Introduction

face that reflect certain light rays while absorbing others. These structures are so small that they cannot be distinguished even with the help of the optical microscope. However, pictures taken with a microscope using beams of electrons have shown us the shape and arrangement of these *submicroscopic* scale structures.

Although there are exceptions, it is safe to say that, by and large, the red, orange, yellow, and brown colors found in butterflies are pigment colors. Blues, violets, and greens are usually of structural origin. While entire families may tend to display one or the other kind of color, there are many species that have a combination of both.

The pigmented scales are really tiny transparent bags filled with a coloring matter that imparts its hue to this container. The coloring matter may be removed by the use of certain chemicals. Pigment colors are frequently subject to fading when exposed to light over long periods of time. Structural colors do not fade, but they can be destroyed by damaging the structures that produce them. The structural scales also contain some pigment, usually dark brown *melanin*, but this pigment serves as a background only and not as coloring matter. The actual color of the scale is produced with the help of tiny ridges and other surface structures. These structures refract, or bend, white light, and reflect only one of its component rays, usually a wave length

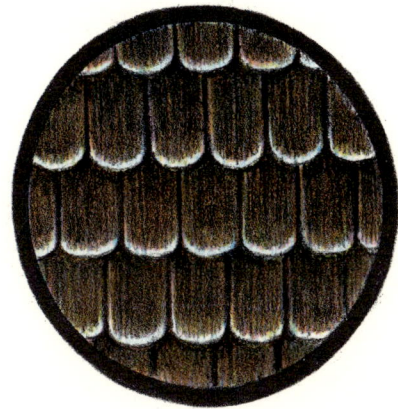

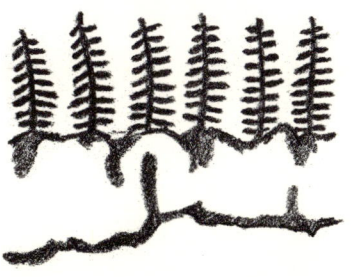

Enlargement of the Morpho scales shows them to be iridescent (left). A slight change of light angle will eliminate the blue color (right). Electronic photograph of scale structures (magnified 25,000 times) shows the ridges that create the blue color.

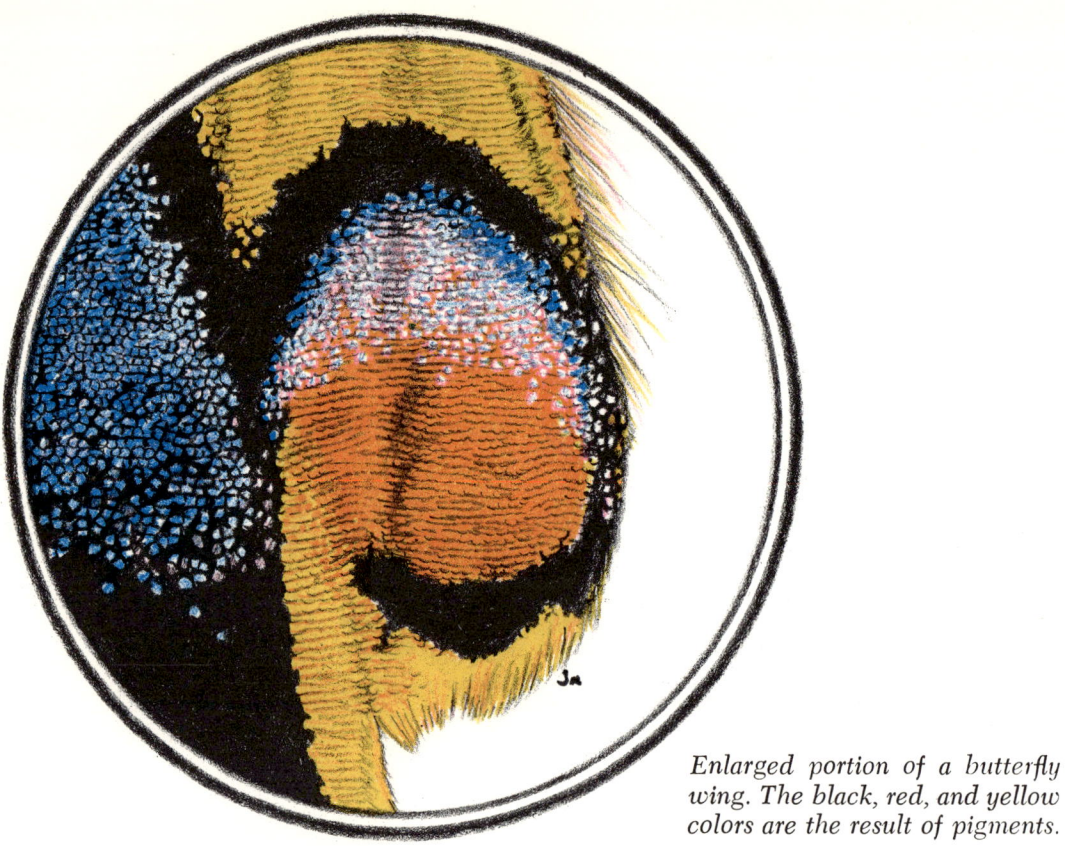

Enlarged portion of a butterfly wing. The black, red, and yellow colors are the result of pigments.

from the green-blue-violet side of the spectrum.

Some of these blue hues are the result of light *diffusion*, or scattering. Much of the blue found in nature, such as that of the sky, blue feathers, and blue eyes, is due to light scattering. The beautiful shimmering blues and violets of many butterflies, especially those of the *Morpho* family, whose glittering wings are used to make jewelry, are produced by a much more complicated optical process called *interference*. Interference colors, which are very pure and brilliant, appear only under certain conditions. In the case of butterfly scales, submicroscopic scale structures are arranged in a way that causes certain wave lengths to neutralize and eliminate one another, so that only one color of the spectrum is reflected. With every change of the light angle, a different color appears: the colors are *iridescent*, meaning that they undergo a rainbow-like play and change of hues.

Introduction

Seen with the naked eye, all scales, structural and pigmental alike, look like tiny specks of colored dust. Enlarged about a dozen times, a portion of a butterfly wing takes on the appearance of a pile rug, owing to the tightly packed rows of overlapping scales. Under a microscope, we can distinguish the individual scales. Attached to the membrane by short stalks, they overlap very much like shingles on a roof.

The Danaids, as milkweed butterflies are called by zoologists, do not have any iridescent colors. Their reds, yellows, browns, and blacks are all pigment colors. Although their bright patterns are often quite handsome, these attractive colors are believed to serve a very special purpose, that of warning would-be attackers. A small family, as butterfly families go, the Danaids are very interesting, and include some unusual members. The North American monarch is, in fact, one of the most famous butterflies in the world.

As the popular family name indicates, Danaids, or rather their larvae, are partial to milkweed. Milkweed belongs to a family of plants called *Asclepiadaceae,* which includes many different species found in various parts of the world. Practically all of these plants have milky, distasteful, often more or less poisonous juices. Not many insects feed

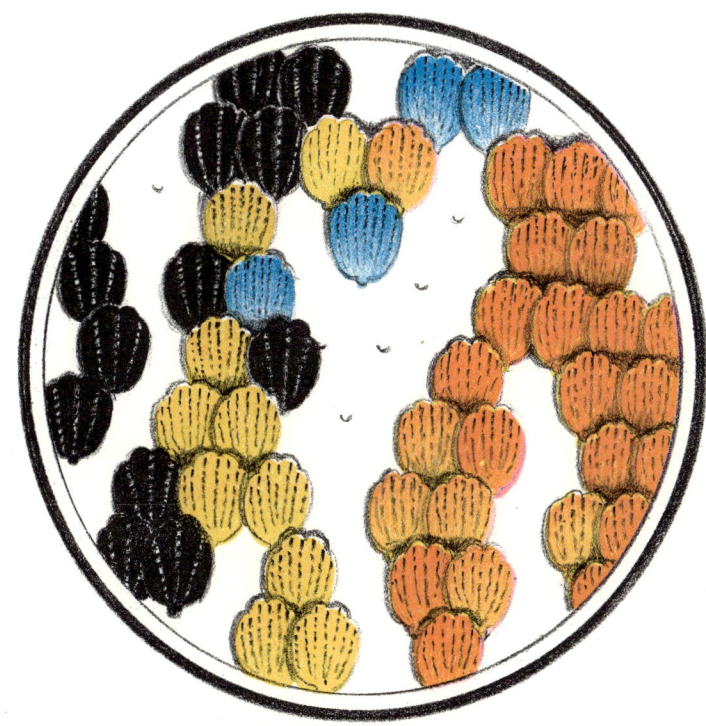

Small portion of preceding illustration, greatly enlarged. Some scales were removed to show how they are fastened to the membrane by their stalks.

Introduction

on milkweed; those that do are often distinguished by brightly colored body patterns, frequently in combinations of red or orange and black.

The caterpillars of the Danaids adhere to this rule. Their colors, usually arranged in a pattern of transverse stripes or rows of spots and featuring contrasting colors such as orange, yellow, white, and black, are very conspicuous as the insects feed on the green milkweed leaves.

Being conspicuous, however, does not seem to bother any member of the tribe, whether immature or adult. Nor does it appear to have any adverse effect on their chances for survival. Most of the milkweed butterflies have eye-catching wing patterns, regardless of variations in color and design. In this group, we do not find the camouflage colors and patterns displayed by so many other butterflies, especially when they sit down to rest and show the undersides of the wings. We also do not find among the Danaids the nervous and hasty behavior typical of most butterflies. Flying about slowly, they show few signs of fear, nor do they try to hide. Their behavior would tempt us to say that they *flaunt* their bright colors if we did not know that butterflies, like all other insects, cannot do anything deliberately as a result of thought. Instead, they follow inborn instincts that tell them what to do, and these instincts quite evidently advise them that they may behave in this unconcerned fashion. Why this is so, how we came to learn about it, why naturalists consider these butterflies and their relatives to be the most advanced members of the entire order, is a fascinating story that will be unfolded in the chapters that follow.

MILKWEED BUTTERFLIES
OF THE TROPICS

Milkweed Butterflies of the Tropics

The tropical regions of the world, which have a wealth of plant and animal life, are the home of the great majority of living insects. Although this fact offers a wide field of opportunity to students of insect life, it will hardly arouse much enthusiasm in the average person, who finds himself beset by a host of flying, crawling, stinging, and biting creatures while living or traveling in these hot countries. The bright side of the picture is supplied by the local Lepidoptera, for they neither sting nor bite, and surely no one with an eye for beauty will remain indifferent to the abundance of large and strikingly colored butterflies found in the equatorial latitudes. Entire families, such as the glittering blue Morphoes of South and Central America, occur only in tropical zones. Others may have a few representatives in the temperate parts of the world, whereas their tropical and subtropical members number in the hundreds.

Our milkweed butterflies are no exception to this rule. Relatively few species — most notably the North American monarch — are found outside the tropics and subtropics. Europe has no native representatives of the family, although the monarch has spread to parts of that continent within the past eighty years and is now fairly well established in England. This enterprising butterfly is also found in other parts of the world — Australia and South America, for example — and naturalists are not quite sure how much of its spread was due to accident, such as transportation of individual insects by ship, and how much was achieved by the monarch traveling under its own power. Be this as it may, the great majority of milkweed butterflies are children of the tropics of both the Old and New worlds.

Because of the great many varieties of Asclepias plants, and the many different localities in which milkweed occurs, tropical Danaids may be found in almost any kind of habitat, ranging from open, sunny meadows and plains to the dank shade of sweltering rain forests. Wherever the butterflies occur, their boldly patterned caterpillars can be seen feeding on the local species of milkweed.

The North American milkweeds, although distasteful to most animals, are at most only mildly poisonous. This, however, is not true of the tropical species, many of which contain potent poison. In Africa, for example, some milkweed plants are used to make arrow poison. In parts of West Africa, the natives mix chopped milkweed roots with grain, so that the birds that eat this bait become unconscious and then can be easily captured. Even large animals may be captured or killed in this way. Hyenas and jackals are known to have died after eating bait meat that had been mixed with chopped milkweed.

Scientists have not yet concluded their studies on the toxicity of the various milkweed species. Some of them are deadly for man. How potent milkweed poison can be was illustrated by the fate of a young Bantu child who ate a grasshopper of a species that feeds on milkweed. The child died twelve hours after he had swallowed the insect. Symptoms of poisoning included vomiting, convulsions, and, finally, paralysis.

This case proves not only the extreme toxicity of certain milkweed poisons, but also the astonishing fact that insects feeding on such plants evidently become as poisonous as the food they consume. These insects, including some milkweed butterflies and related species, are able to store the poison in their bodies without poisoning themselves, though the poison retains its capacity for harm. The intriguing question, of course, is how these butterflies manage to retain in their systems, throughout the subsequent stages of metamorphosis, the poison consumed by their caterpillars. Scientists at one time thought the answer to this puzzle was that the caterpillars accumulate the poison in their intestines. That theory, however, does not account for the fact that the adult insects, which have changed their food preferences and live only on nectar, are as poisonous as the caterpillars. Also, not only the intestinal tracts but every part of the body of these insects is poisonous, indicating that the toxic substances are present in all the body tissues. It therefore must be assumed that the caterpillars, through some wizardry of their body chemistry, have a special way of accumulating the poison molecules in their tissues. Apparently the molecules remain stored in the tissues without disintegrating, and are not affected by the fundamental body changes occurring during the metamorphosis that transforms the caterpillar into a butterfly. Studies on just how this is accomplished by the insects' body chemistry are continuing.

Not all milkweed butterflies, of course, are actually poisonous. Depending upon the qualities of the Asclepias species their caterpillars feed on, most of them are probably no more than distasteful. Even that, however, means that they are not good to eat for most insect-eating animals, and that, in turn, is very important for the but-

Orient

Africa-India

Indo-Australia

Indo-Australia

India

Indo-Australia

Old-World species of milkweed butterflies

This subspecies of the African monarch has lost most of the color in the hind wings.

terflies. Close observation of these handsome butterflies and various tests and experiments have produced evidence that the Danaids are shunned by many insectivores, primarily birds. Inexperienced birds will try to eat them, but usually reject them quickly. After a few of such — quite literally bitter — experiences the bird learns to recognize the pattern and coloring of the unpalatable butterflies and thereafter cannot be induced to sample another of this kind. It is thus apparent that the bright, conspicuous patterns of distasteful insects serve a definite purpose: easy to recognize, they are warning signals advertising the fact that their owners are distasteful, or even poisonous. Because of this, it may well be advantageous for the inedible insects to openly display their bright "warning" colors, as so many of them do. In this way, they gain immunity from attack by those predators that associate the bright pattern with previous unpleasant experiences.

Seen from our viewpoint, the trouble with this immunity is that so many butterflies have to be killed or mutilated before insectivores of a given region are "educated" and learn to recognize the patterns. In nature, however, protection and survival of the species, not the individual, is what is essential. Many butterflies die in the "educating" process, but the species as a whole benefits, and the surviving members enjoy a life of comparative freedom and security: they are "protected" butterflies.

This protection, of course, is always only partial. Some animals will eat practically any insect, regardless of how distasteful it may be to others. Still, even partial protection is a tremendous advantage. The bold and unconcerned behavior of the milkweed butterflies seems to be a clear indication that their advertised inedibility does indeed afford them a good measure of immunity.

By far the best-known and most widespread of the African milkweed butterflies is *Danaus chrysippus*, the golden Danaid, also often called the African monarch. This butterfly, or one of its many subspecies, can be found over an area extending all the way from Africa to India and Australia. Its appearance fully justifies its name, for the predominant color is a warm, bright golden-brown. The tips of the forewings are black with white spots, and the hind wings also have a few black spots as well as a black border. The subspecies display many variations of this basic color theme. *Danaus chrysippus dorippus*, for instance, lacks the black-and-white wing tips, while *Danaus chrysippus alcippus* has lost most of the brown color in the hind wings, which thus appear predominantly white, except for a thin brown edging inside the black border. Such color variations create new and eye-catching combinations without fundamentally changing the basic pattern or introducing new colors.

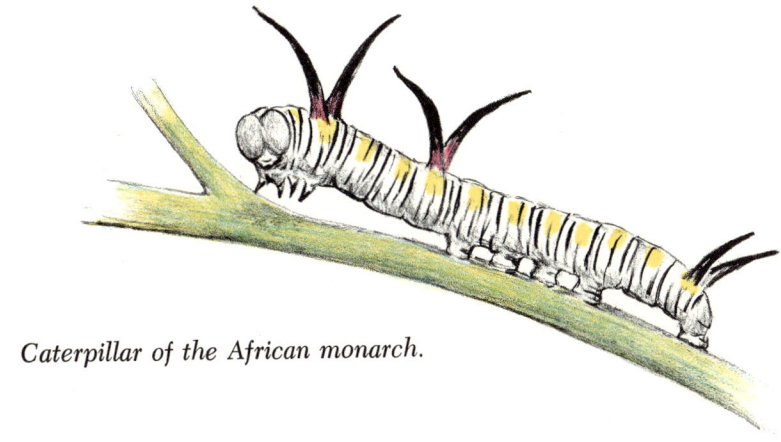

Caterpillar of the African monarch.

The African monarch is a creature of the open plains, especially of South Africa, where, as a handsome caterpillar, brightly colored in black and yellow, like all milkweed larvae, it feeds on the local species of Asclepias.

In the typically bold manner of all the Danaids, the African monarch ventures into the open, away from all shelter, and flies about slowly, keeping a straight course during flight without much fluttering or flapping of wings. This, by the way, is an aid in identifying this butterfly on the wing, for unrelated butterflies occurring in the same region are striking "doubles" of the African monarch as far as appearance is concerned but give themselves away by their different manner of flight.

The golden Danaid prefers the sunny open spaces, but other African members of the family prefer the shade and are found in wooded areas, some even in the dense depths of the tropical rain forests. Many of these species look very different from the golden-brown *Danaus chrysippus*. Butterflies of the genus *Amauris*, for example, a forest-dwelling, shade-loving group, have bold patterns of black or very dark brown with large patches of white. Sometimes these patches are bluish and have a slight opalescence.

Like the golden Danaid, the *Amauris* butterflies have some remarkable doubles among butterflies of other, unrelated families. Here again, the leisurely, unhurried flight of the milkweed butterflies is helpful for identifying them in the air. Slowness of flight may be even more pronounced in the *Amauris* species than in other members of the family. Watching an *Amauris* butterfly sailing along slowly and examining everything that caught its fancy, one observer was reminded of a little old lady enjoying herself on a leisurely window-shopping trip.

In addition to their bold, conspicuous patterns, these butterflies have another protective feature: they emit a strong, acrid odor, a hint of their bitter-tasting body juices. Enemies are therefore warned by sight *and* smell that they are wise if they do not try to make a snack of these insects. One naturalist has called the black-and-white *Amauris* species the "skunks among the butterflies," and indeed there is some basis for the analogy. The skunk, too, is an animal that moves around slowly, secure in the knowledge of the excellent protection it possesses, an immunity advertised by its bold, distinctive black-and-white body pattern.

Leaving Africa and moving on to India, we again meet the golden Danaid. Nicknamed the "tiger" because of the orange-black-white pattern of the undersides of its wings, it is a fairly common butterfly but only one of the many Danaids found in the Indo-Australian region. These species vary greatly in size, pattern, and coloring. Some are relatively small, others may have a wingspread of more than four inches, with bold patterns usually featuring combinations of orange, brown, black, and white. *Danaus leonippus indicus* has a pattern of black and white with large patches of orange at the base of its forewings. Another species displays the identical pattern except that it lacks the orange patches.

In some of the Indo-Australian species, portions of the wing may be partly transparent, meaning that the scale covering in those spots is thin or missing altogether, so that the wing membrane is exposed. Large, handsome *Danaus tytia nephonica* has a pattern consisting of various shades of brown and partially transparent white. The much smaller *Danaus schenkii periphas* also has partly transparent wing areas, but these are tinted a delicate yellow, while the rest of the wing is black.

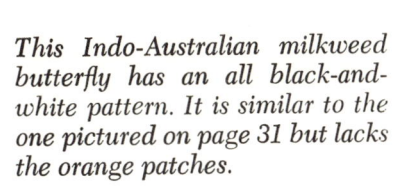

This Indo-Australian milkweed butterfly has an all black-and-white pattern. It is similar to the one pictured on page 31 but lacks the orange patches.

A species of Euploea. In color and pattern, these butterflies differ considerably from the "monarch type" milkweed butterfly.

Butterflies of the genus *Euploea* have a coloring that is somewhat similar to that of the *Amauris* species, although the pattern and the wing shape are different. Black or dark brown with white spots, some of the *Euploea* have an opalescent blue sheen over large parts of the wing area. And the genus *Danaida* has departed completely from the "typical" colors of the milkweed family; here we find butterflies with pale blue and black wing patterns.

Whatever the appearance of the Danaids, however, they are all "brothers under the skin," and very much alike in typical features, food preference of the caterpillars, and a degree of immunity because of their distastefulness.

Not only Africa and the Indo-Australian regions but also the tropical and subtropical zones of the Western Hemisphere can boast of a large number of native milkweed butterflies. A more diverse and interesting lot than these Central and South American Danaids and their close relatives would be difficult to find. Here, as in the Old World, the various species of milkweed butterflies may be found in many different habitats, ranging from the open plains to the dense shade of jungle forests whose depths are rarely penetrated by the rays of the sun.

Some of the South American Danaids have the typical "monarch" pattern and appearance. Not only the tropical subspecies of the

Milkweed Butterflies of the Tropics

monarch but also a number of others display the orange or brown wings with black veins and borders and white spots. Others, however, look entirely different, and a few, such as the genera *Ituna* and *Lycorea,* not only have different patterns but also wing shapes and body proportions different from the usual member of the family. These species do, however, look very much like the members of two other, closely related groups, the Ithomiids and Heliconiids. All these butterflies are more or less distinguished by rather narrow wings and long abdomens. When their wings are fully spread, their abdomens extend far beyond the wing area. In some of the more extreme examples, these butterflies look more like dragonflies or damselflies than Lepidoptera.

Because quite a few species of milkweed butterflies resemble the Ithomiid and Heliconiid families — and vice versa — identifications would be difficult even without further complications. However, just

The difference in wing and body proportions between the monarch-type and certain New-World milkweed butterflies is illustrated in this diagram.

Central America

South America

Brazil

Panama-Peru

South America

Panama

Various species of New-World milkweed butterflies

to make things more confusing, some Danaids look different in different localities, resembling in all cases the local species of the related groups. In addition, a number of other, unrelated butterflies belonging to different families also display the same patterns, shapes, and colors. Collectors thus may easily end up with half a dozen butterflies that all look alike but belong to different species and families, some of them distasteful, others not.

It was precisely this incredibly confusing situation which, about a hundred years ago, set naturalists thinking about a possible explanation for this resemblance among different butterflies. In the next chapter, we shall discuss some of the interesting facts they uncovered and how the theories they advanced provided an acceptable solution to the "Case of the Confusing Butterflies."

THE WONDERS OF MIMICRY

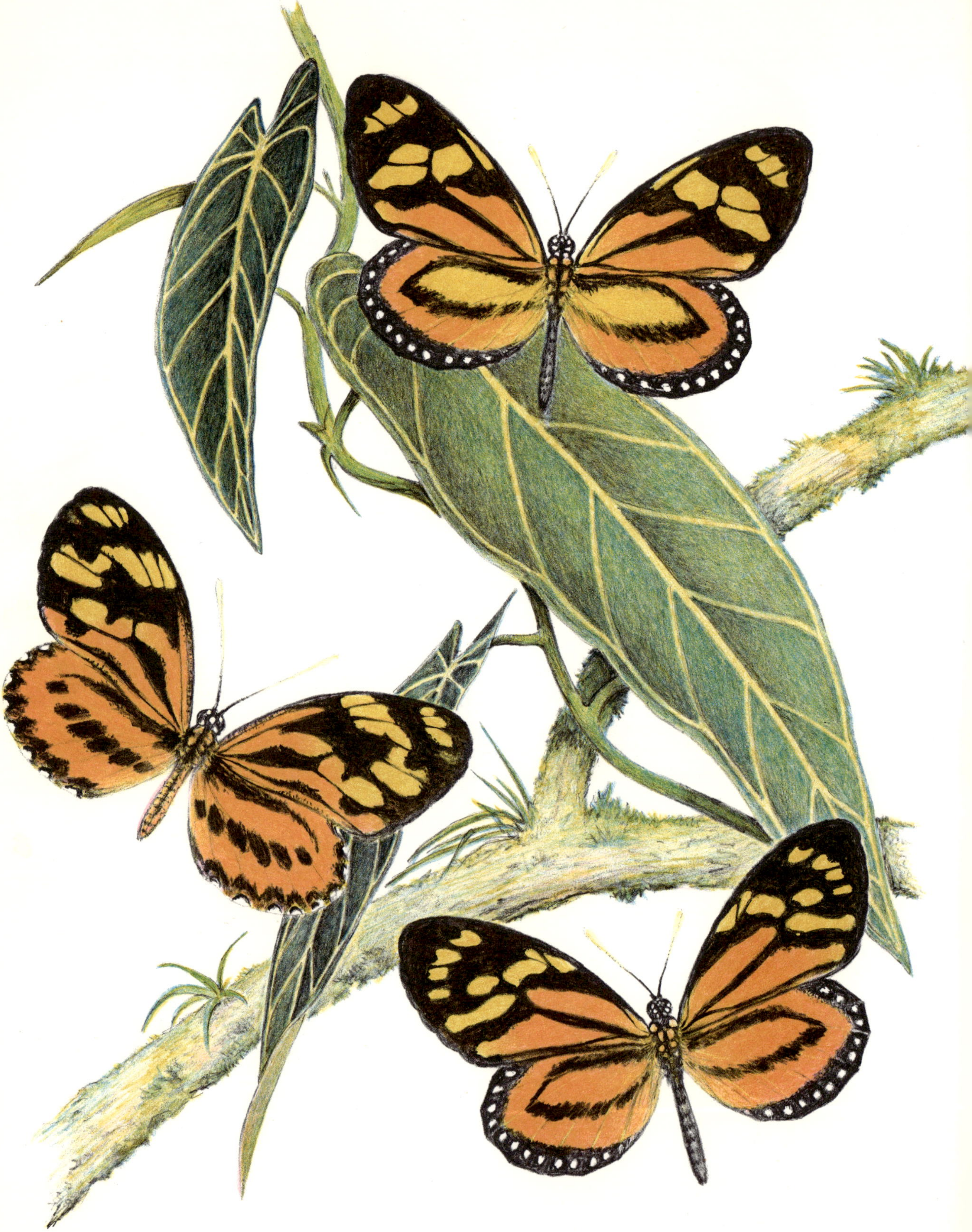

The Wonders of Mimicry

What is mimicry? To mimic means to imitate, and when we say that one person mimics another, we are saying that he or she imitates the other person's appearance, way of talking, walking, laughing, or other characteristics. The mimic tries to reproduce his "model's" behavior and mannerisms. In zoology, the word mimicry has a somewhat different meaning, for it nearly always involves appearance only, and is used in cases in which one animal looks very much like another, different animal. Loosely speaking, it may even be applied to the close resemblance of an animal to an inanimate object, such as a stone, or to twigs, leaves, or flowers.

The Wonders of Mimicry

The dictionary defines zoological mimicry as "the superficial resemblance that an animal exhibits to other animals, or to the natural objects among which it lives, thereby securing concealment, protection, and the like." Zoologists today, however, generally do not use the term mimicry in those instances where animals *conceal* themselves by resembling natural objects. This kind of imitation is called camouflage, its aim being to protect the imitators against discovery by enemy eyes. In mimicry, as it is commonly understood today, camouflage does not enter the picture — on the contrary, both models and mimics are often brightly and conspicuously colored and do not even attempt to conceal themselves.

The big difference between human and animal mimicry is, of course, the fact that the animal does not *know* it is imitating a model, does not do so deliberately, and would in any case be unable to do anything else. Controlled by instinct and not by reason, insects, among which mimicry is chiefly found, look and act the way they do without any conscious knowledge of why and how they do it.

The stick insect's shape and coloring give it a perfect camouflage.

The Wonders of Mimicry

Mimicry is a fascinating and somewhat controversial phenomenon. Many aspects of mimicry are puzzles whose solutions still evade us, leaving countless questions unanswered. So far, zoologists have failed to agree among themselves on some important points. In both camouflage and "true" mimicry, the difficulty centers mainly on one question: how did the process begin? In other words, what and how was the starting point of a change of body shape or color — or both — which ended in the "mimic's" close resemblance to a leaf, a twig, a flower, or an insect of an entirely different family. That all these resemblances are purely coincidental can be practically ruled out, but what triggered them remains a mystery. For the time being, we have to be content with marveling at the perfection of detail in some of these insect disguises, such as the stick and leaf insects, or the tropical praying mantis that looks exactly like a pink orchid blossom.

Mimicry in the strict zoological sense — imitation, by one insect, of the shape, colors, and pattern of a different insect — is found in a wide variety of cases. Almost invariably, the insect "model" is naturally well protected, either by formidable weapons such as poison stings, or by obnoxious body juices that render it inedible to many insect-eating animals. Also, almost invariably, these models are marked with conspicuous body patterns and bright colors, often in combinations of black and red or yellow. In this connection it is interesting to note that these colors — yellow, orange, and red — are widely used by man to call attention to possible danger and to warn him to be careful. Traffic lights, school buses, and construction signals are a few examples of our warning colors. Familiar well-protected and well-marked insects are hornets and bumblebees. After a few painful or "bitter" experiences, birds and other insectivores will learn to stay away from such prey. It follows that if an unarmed "edible" insect looks very much like a "protected" species, predators that have had unpleasant encounters with the models will also stay away from the mimics. This theory seems to be borne out by the fact that many different unarmed insects such as flies, moths, and beetles mimic wasps and bumblebees.

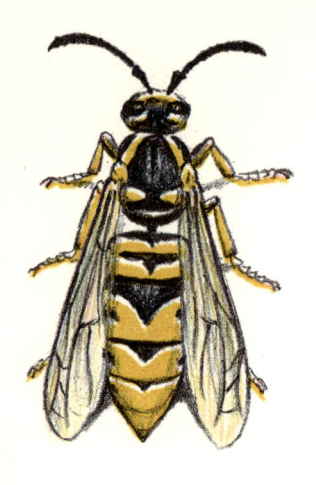

Moth (right) is an excellent mimic, both in design and color, of the well-armed hornet (left).

Wasp mimics are especially numerous. Many different species of flies, for instance, have the conspicuous yellow-and-black patterns of hornets. So does the locust borer, a beetle found in many parts of North America. Probably one of the most striking hornet mimics is the hornet clear-wing moth, which has departed far from the typical appearance of its group in having slender wings with very little scale covering and a body which in shape, coloring, and pattern manages to present a very good likeness of a large hornet. Another moth mimics a bumblebee, and so do several flies. Even grasshoppers can be wasp mimics: one tropical species resembles in all details the reddish-brown, yellow-and-black color pattern of a local wasp.

For the layman, it is often impossible to distinguish between the real thing and the imitator; small wonder, then, that a bird is unable to tell the difference. This means, of course, that the mimic gets a definite and appreciable protection through its resemblance to a genuinely protected insect. As in the case of the model, the immunity of the mimic is always only partial, but even that is a great boon to an otherwise defenseless creature.

Mimicry is a comparatively new field of study. It began about one hundred years ago in the wake of Charles Darwin's theory of evolution, which is largely based on the theory of "natural selection." Darwin thought he had found evidence in nature that only animals which are

The Wonders of Mimicry

well equipped and adapted to their environment can withstand and overcome the dangers of everyday life and have a chance for survival. Others, not fit enough to prevail in the struggle for existence, fall by the wayside and become extinct. Darwin's contention that this concept of the "survival of the fittest" is at the core of the entire evolutionary process was a convincing argument in view of the adaptive features displayed by so many animals. Today, some zoologists are no longer entirely satisfied that the natural-selection theory can explain all the phenomena in the animal kingdom. They point to animals that survive and flourish despite features that seem to hinder rather than help them. These scientists are looking for additional answers to the enigma of evolution. Whatever the answer, a century ago Darwin's revolutionary theories stimulated a tremendous new interest in all animal life, with the result that many fascinating new facts were uncovered.

Darwin's contemporary, the naturalist Alfred R. Wallace, was struck by the bright and often garish colors displayed by certain insects, colors that contrasted sharply with their natural surroundings and tended to make these creatures look conspicuous rather than help conceal them. Despite such exposure, however, these insects seemed to enjoy a remarkable immunity to attack by insect-eating animals such as birds and monkeys. Far from hurting their chances of survival, their attention-inviting colors actually appeared to help them. After more investigation, the naturalist came to the conclusion that these insects were apparently unsuited as food for other animals, being either poi-

Moth (right) mimics the distasteful orange-and-black beetle (left).

This Central American Danaid is well protected by its distasteful body juices.

sonous or evil-tasting. Observers noted that young and inexperienced monkeys would taste these insects, discard them, and after a few such attempts would shy away from them altogether. Quite evidently these monkeys had become "educated," meaning that they had come to remember and recognize the distinctive pattern and color combination as a signal warning them of an unpleasant taste experience.

Further research disclosed the surprising fact that a number of the insects with "warning" patterns were not really unpalatable. They only looked like the truly distasteful species. The resemblance was in many cases so close that it was impossible, even for the expert, to tell the model and the mimic apart without closely examining them.

The first serious study of this particular kind of mimicry was made by the English naturalist Henry W. Bates, another contemporary and correspondent of Darwin. Bates spent a great deal of time collecting butterflies in the Amazon region of South America during the middle of the last century. After he got home with his collection, he began the task of sorting out his specimens. To his surprise, he found upon

The Wonders of Mimicry

closer inspection that a number of butterflies, which he had taken to be members of the same species because they looked so much alike, belonged, in reality, to different groups!

Some of these butterflies were female members of the family *Pierinae*, popularly called Whites. Our all-too-common and familiar white cabbage butterfly, whose caterpillar is a serious pest of cabbage, belongs in this group, which is widespread and has representatives in many parts of the world. The female Whites collected by Bates did not, however, resemble the typical White in shape or color, nor did they even look like the males of their own species. They had departed completely from their ancestral patterns and colors to become conspicuously colored in bright yellow, red, and black, with wing and body shapes that closely resembled those of their distasteful models! The latter were members of the earlier-mentioned *Ithomiidae*, relatives of the monarch. Like the milkweed butterflies, the Ithomiids as caterpillars feed on evil-tasting plants and are unpalatable in all stages of metamorphosis.

This strong resemblance of "edible" butterflies (Whites are readily eaten by birds and other insectivores) to inedible kinds started Bates off on the development of a theory that later was to become known as "Batesian mimicry." Basically, this theory centers on the con-

This perfectly edible butterfly mimics colors and patterns of the distasteful Danaid on the opposite page.

tention that unprotected insects, by resembling genuinely protected species, share in the immunity of their evil-tasting or well-armed models.

Studies similar to those that Bates had used as a basis for his theory were later conducted by other naturalists with butterflies in Africa and the Orient. In Africa, especially, there are some fascinating cases of mimicry involving Danaid models. Two species of the forest-dwelling *Amauris*, for instance, are mimicked by two species of the genus *Hypolimnas*, edible butterflies belonging to the large and worldwide family *Nymphalidae*, which includes such familiar butterflies as the North American red admiral and the European purple emperor.

An interesting feature of the *Hypolimnas* case, as well as many other cases of butterfly mimicry, is that only the females display the false "warning" colors, whereas the males retain the ancestral pattern of their kind. An especially striking difference exists between the males of *Hypolimnas misippus*, which are black with a large blue-tinted spot on each wing, and the mimetic females. The latter have departed completely from the pattern and coloration of their kind; instead, they are striking "doubles" of *Danaus chrysippus*, the African monarch described earlier in this book. Male and female *Hypolimnas misippus* thus do not resemble each other at all, and it is difficult to believe that these two are indeed members of the same species.

The difference in appearance between the sexes, called *dimorphism* by biologists, is a phenomenon frequently found among animals. Usually, however, the female is more drab-looking than the male. In the case of the female butterflies that mimic protected species, it is just the other way around: the female is more strikingly colored than the male.

Possibly the most interesting case of mimicry by female butterflies of an "edible" species is found in Africa and involves a local species of swallowtail. *Papilio dardanus* occurs widely over large areas of the African mainland and Madagascar. The males always display the typical coloring of their species, in this case black markings and borders with large areas of creamy white. They also have the swallowtail shape, with little tails on the hind wings. The females, however, look quite different, for they mimic various Danaids. One naturalist has called *Papilio dardanus* the "most interesting butterfly in the world," and even though this may be an exaggeration, there can be no doubt that this species has provided us with one of the most intriguing examples of mimicry. The model of the female *Papilio dardanus* is the African monarch — quite evidently a fashionable model in butterfly circles — and we find that its various subspecies are mimicked by the subspecies of our African swallowtail. The exception to this rule is a non-mimetic subspecies of *Papilio dardanus* in Madagascar. Here, females and males look alike, and both look like swallowtails. Naturalists think that these butterflies probably suffered less from predators than did their relatives in other parts of Africa.

Although it may seem peculiar that mimicry of a protected species occurs so frequently among female butterflies only, biologists offer a logical explanation for this fact. The females — biologically the more valuable sex — need the protection because they are more exposed to attack, especially while engaged in egg-laying. The males, not handicapped in this way, have a better chance of escaping a predator.

In the course of their studies of Batesian mimicry, naturalists found evidence that a number of protected species mimic other protected kinds belonging to different groups. When this occurred, it was difficult to say which was the model and which the mimic. Possible reasons for this kind of mimicry were investigated by Fritz Müller, a German naturalist who lived in Brazil and who, like Wallace and Bates, frequently corresponded with Darwin.

Brazil was a perfect place for such studies, for here Müller could find a great many protected butterflies all belonging to different groups, but all mimicking one another. On the strength of his findings, he evolved a theory concerning mimicry among protected insects only. This theory later became known as "Müllerian mimicry" because, although it supplements Batesian mimicry, it differs from the latter in many respects.

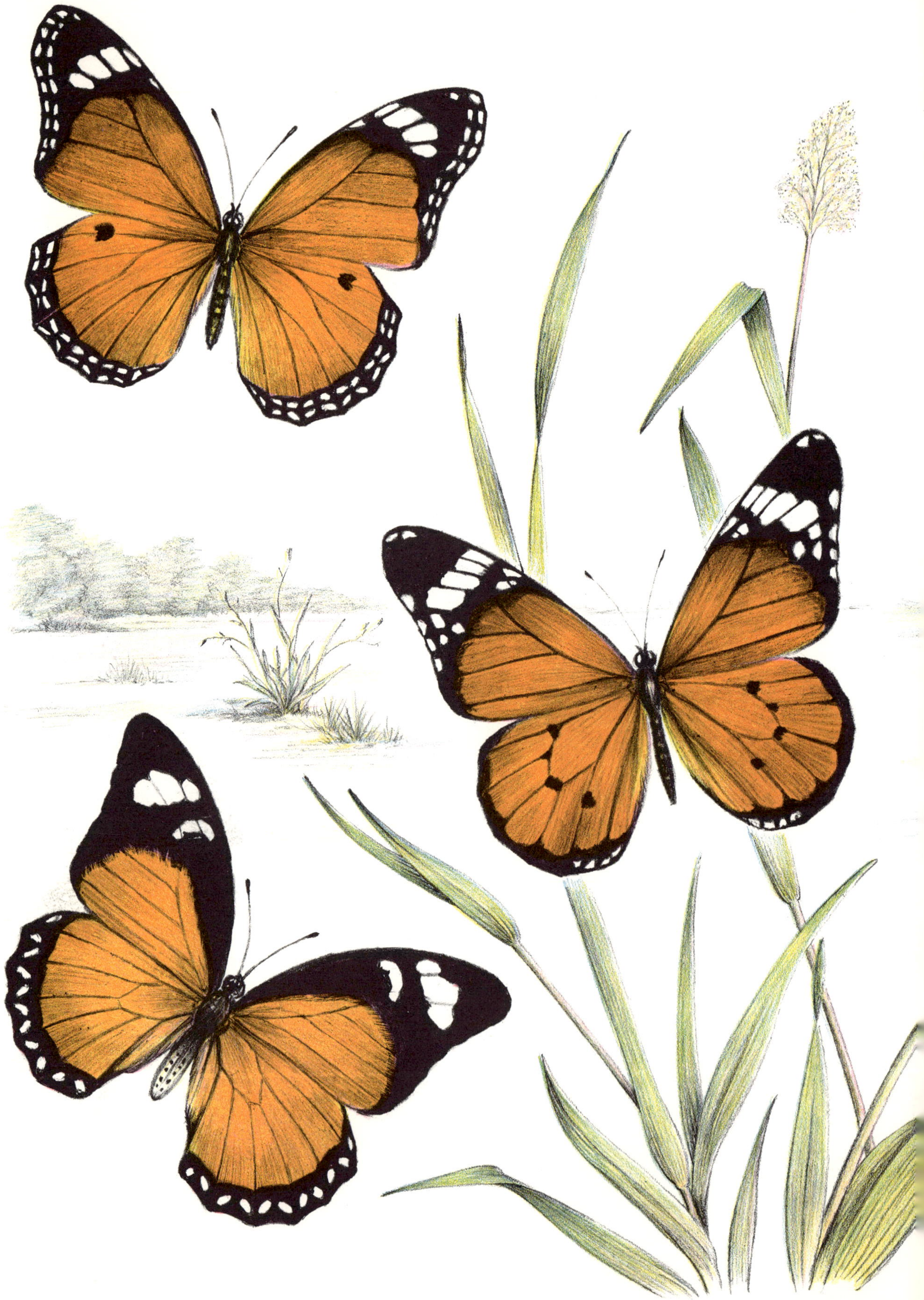

The African monarch is mimicked by many butterflies. Often, as here, only the females mimic the distasteful species, while the males retain the ancestral colors and patterns of their kind. Females of both Papilio dardanus *and* Hypolimnas misippus *(upper and lower left) show color patterns similar to those of* Danaus chrysippus *(center). Males of both species look quite different (right).*

Müller's theory consisted mainly of the contention that if two or more inedible species look very much alike, they will share in, and considerably cut down on, the inevitable losses occurring during the "training" period of young and inexperienced insectivores. Let us assume, for example, that a given region has a population of three different kinds of distasteful butterflies, and that species A numbers 10,000, species B, 6,000, and species C, 9,000 individuals. Assuming also that inexperienced animals such as birds and monkeys will have to destroy 1,500 individuals before they learn to recognize a single pattern, it follows that groups A, B, and C will each lose 1,500 members if these three groups all look different. If, on the other hand, they bear a striking resemblance to one another, the loss would be shared by all three collectively, more or less in proportion to their number. Müller's theory that it is advantageous for protected species to engage in mimicry seems to be borne out by the facts.

Because both kinds of mimicry are found occurring together among butterflies that include South American Danaids and their relatives, milkweed butterflies are favorite subjects for this kind of research. Many aspects of it are still controversial, but there seems to be no doubt that insect mimics profit from their resemblance to unpalatable or dangerous models, just as other insects profit from camouflage patterns, colors, and shapes that permit them to blend into their background and surroundings. It is easy to see and understand the reasons for mimicry and why it would prove useful to insects without any other kind of defense. That does not mean, however, that we can explain the origin of this phenomenon. As mentioned earlier, we do not know how it began; we do not know what triggered the changes in patterns and color — and frequently shape — that make the members of one species resemble a different, usually unrelated, kind. But we do not need to know the answers to the puzzles of mimicry to marvel at this evidence of yet another of the countless ways in which nature's defenseless creatures are aided in their never-ending struggle for survival.

INTRODUCING THE MONARCH

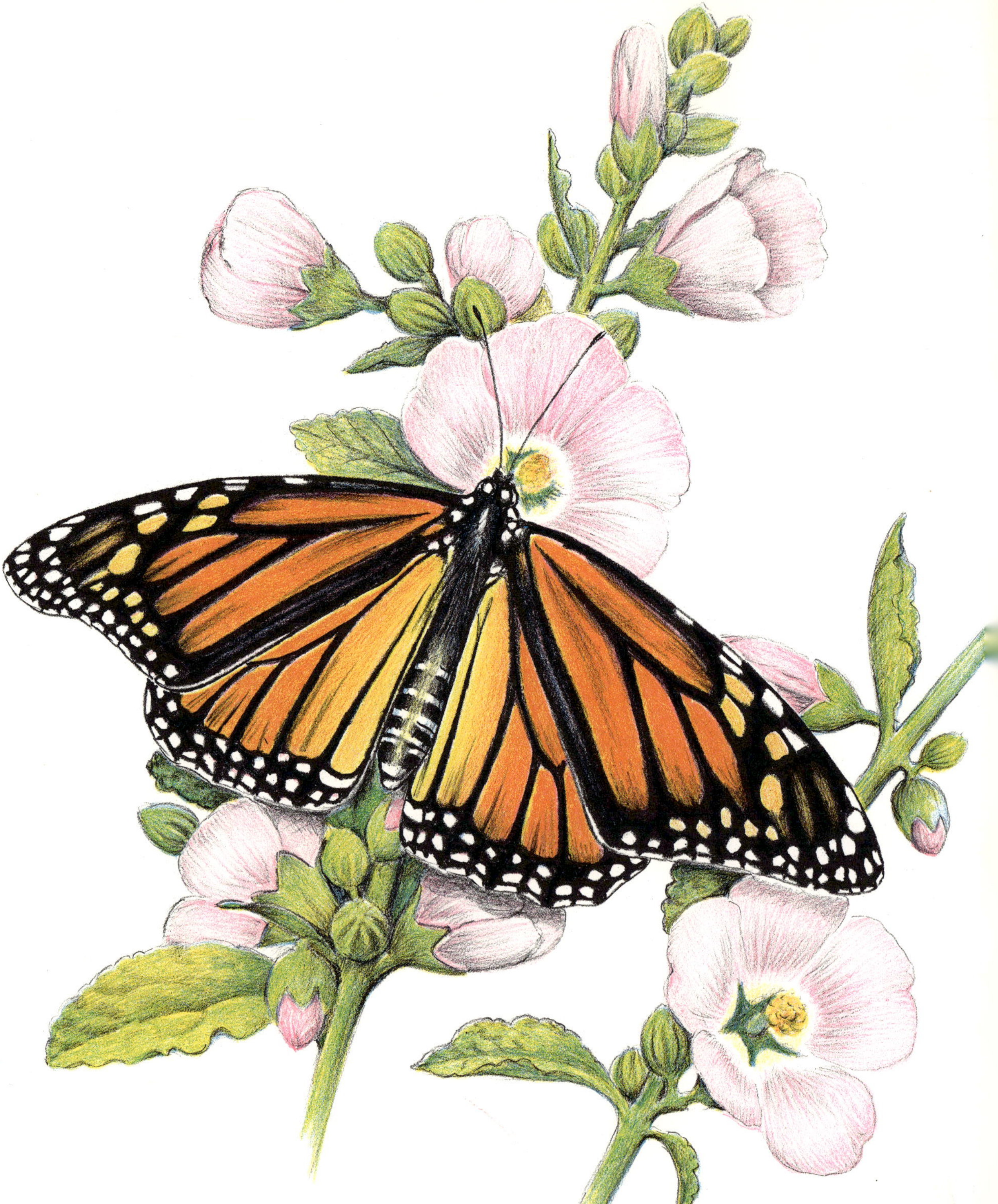

Introducing the Monarch

Among the hundreds of different kinds of butterflies found in North America, possibly none is as universally known as the large, striking monarch. Those who have never seen this handsome, black-and-orange butterfly gliding slowly and majestically through the air are at least familiar with its picture, for the monarch is rarely left out of even the smallest and most limited book on North American insects. Also, this butterfly is frequently shown as the most familiar example of warning coloration mimicked by an "unprotected" species.

In all its actions, the monarch has a truly regal, serene, unhurried, and unconcerned manner. Never displaying the hasty, nervous movement or the shyness typical of many other Lepidoptera, the monarch takes its time, flying about slowly with a good deal of soaring and

Introducing the Monarch

sailing. Stopping to sample a flower here, another there, the monarch will alight on anything that may catch its fancy, including parts of the human anatomy, as sun bathers occasionally find out. One sun enthusiast, who had a camera handy, took some fine pictures of a monarch perching on his big toe, which for some reason had at that time seemed an object worthy of investigation by the bold butterfly.

The monarch's unconcerned behavior is typical of its group and consistent with the fact that, like all other Danaids, it enjoys a certain measure of protection against insect-eating animals because of its distasteful body juices. Its slow and deliberate flight and its tendency to stay out in the open where it can be clearly seen are therefore not really as danger-inviting as it would seem.

The monarch, with its four-inch wingspread, is one of the largest of the North American butterflies. Only the giant swallowtail, which is fairly common in the southeastern areas of the United States, where its larvae feed on the leaves of citrus fruit, has a wingspread of more than four inches.

The monarch's distinctive wing pattern of bright orange, with black veins and wing borders, the latter spotted with white, appears much paler and more brownish on the undersides. The body is a rich, velvety black, with a few white spots on the head and thorax. The velvet effect is caused by a furlike body-covering of fine, short hairs. The long legs are also black. Like others of its group, the monarch has only four functional legs, the two forelegs being quite short and folded against the thorax so that they are hardly visible. The body is tough and rubbery, and it can withstand abuse that would kill most other butterflies. This toughness is also a distinguishing feature of many genuinely protected species.

Wherever milkweed is abundant, monarchs are fairly sure to be around. It is fortunate that the various species of *Asclepias* occurring in North America are found in many different localities. These weeds grow in meadows and fields, along roadsides, and in empty lots. However, destruction of wilderness areas through the expansion of cities

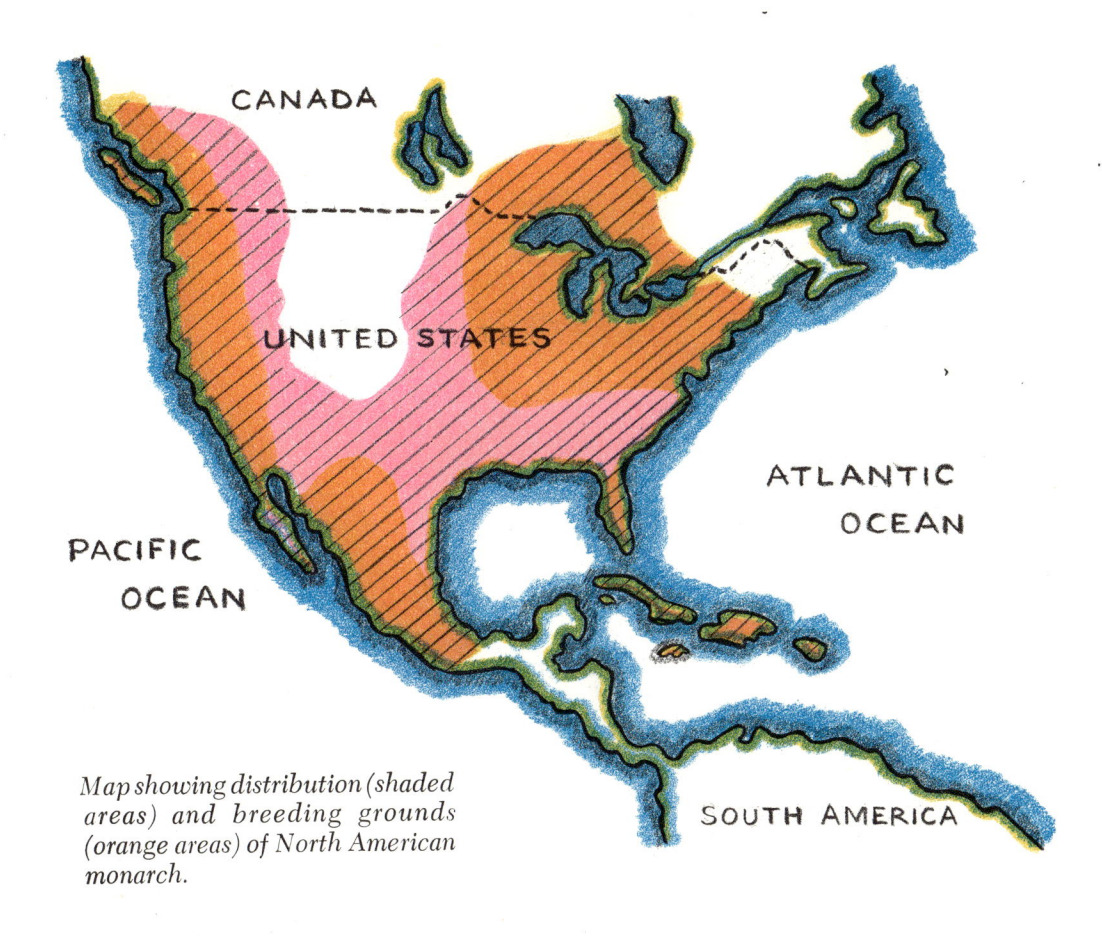

Map showing distribution (shaded areas) and breeding grounds (orange areas) of North American monarch.

and industries has eliminated, along with the habitat of many other small wild creatures, the food plants of many butterflies in large parts of the country. In addition, these beautiful insects have probably suffered more than any others from the extensive — and often indiscriminate — use of insecticides that has become a feature of modern life. Whereas many true insect pests, including mosquitoes and roaches, seem to develop an amazing immunity to most pesticides, and frequently come back each year almost as numerous but tougher than before, butterflies are evidently extremely vulnerable to these poisons, and their population has decreased considerably over the past thirty years. This also holds true for the monarch. It seems quite possible, and indeed probable, that the huge swarms of monarchs that were observed as recently as a decade or so ago have become a thing of the

59

The viceroy is smaller than the monarch but has similar coloring and pattern.

past. This is indeed a great loss. A flock of thousands of these large, brightly colored butterflies on the wing is an overwhelming and inspiring sight. A concerted effort should be made by everyone who values our natural treasures to encourage measures which would increase the present butterfly population in general, and the monarch population in particular. In addition to their being handsome and interesting, these butterflies are also "harmless" from the human point of view. Milkweed, the exclusive food of the monarch caterpillar, has no economic or agricultural importance.

Although the monarch is most famous for its seasonal migrations, details of which will be discussed later, it is also often cited as North Amer-

Introducing the Monarch

ica's most outstanding butterfly "model." It almost invariably appears side by side with its mimic, the viceroy, in any book dealing with the phenomenon of mimicry. The similarity of these two butterflies is quite remarkable. Anyone unfamiliar with every detail of their wing patterns can easily confuse them, for both color and pattern are very much the same except for a black stripe that runs across the veins on the hind wings of the viceroy, which the monarch does not have. The viceroy is also smaller, but comparative size is difficult to determine in the field unless both butterflies are seen close together, which rarely happens. Judging from tests with blue jays, which are known to eat practically anything, there seems to be little doubt that once birds learn to shun the monarch, they also stay away from the viceroy.

In North America, monarchs are found in the entire eastern half of the continent, as well as west of the Rocky Mountains, with the exception of only the northern regions of Canada. They do, however, get up as far as the Hudson Bay area. The only other native North American Danaid, the queen, is not nearly so widely distributed as her larger

The queen is the only other native North American milkweed butterfly.

Introducing the Monarch

cousin, being confined mainly to the southwestern parts of the United States. The queen is smaller and less striking than the monarch. Its wings are more brownish, the black veins less pronounced, and the white spots smaller, more numerous, and arranged in different patterns.

The queen differs from the monarch not only in appearance but also in habit. Like most butterflies, the queen spends its entire life more or less in the same vicinity. Adult butterflies often die not far from the spot where they hatched from the eggs as tiny caterpillars.

Monarchs are different. Although many adults also live and die within a few miles of their "birthplace," others live to travel hundreds of miles to far-off places. A small caterpillar feeding on a milkweed plant way up north in the Hudson Bay region during August may very well, as an adult, enjoy the mild breezes and the sunshine of Florida in the winter months.

Before further exploring the monarch's amazing travels, let us first follow our butterfly through the fascinating stages of its metamorphosis.

THE CATERPILLAR

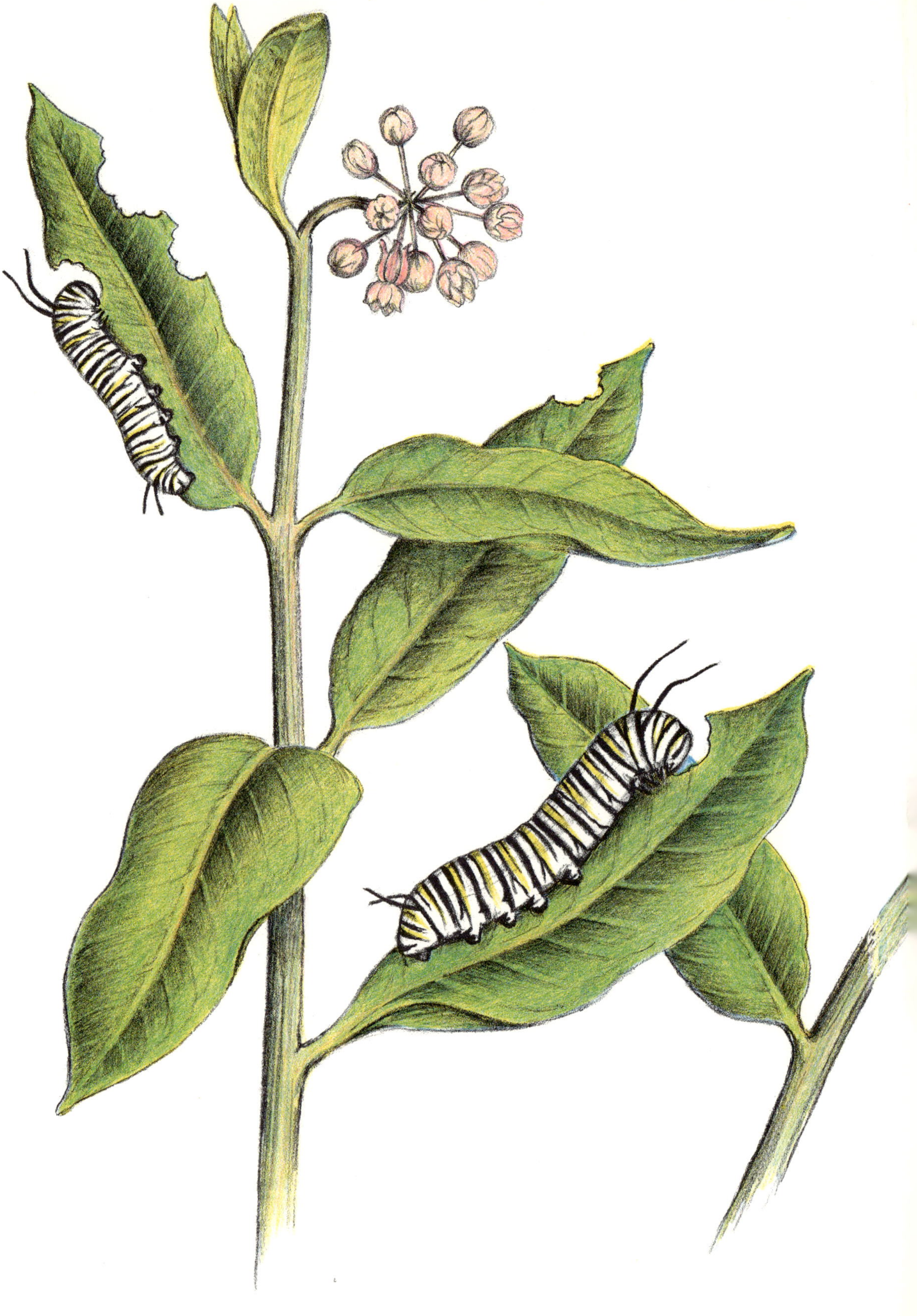

The Caterpillar

The life cycle of the monarch, like that of all butterflies, begins one summer day when the female gets ready to lay her eggs. Butterflies must be careful to pick the right plant on which to deposit their eggs, for caterpillars are extremely choosy about their food. Most of them will eat only one specific kind, refusing all others even if doing so means starvation.

In the case of the monarch, the food plant is any one of the various North American milkweed species. The female glues her eggs, singly or in small groups, usually to the undersides of tender young milkweed leaves. The way she goes about selecting the leaves that will have to

Monarch eggs, greatly enlarged.

serve as food for her newly hatched offspring seems to indicate that monarchs have rather acute eyesight.

A female monarch may lay up to several hundred eggs during her lifetime, but she never deposits more than a few on any one plant. This is typical of all butterflies and distinguishes their eggs from those of moths, which are laid in large clusters or packets sometimes numbering in the hundreds.

Greatly magnified, the monarch egg looks very dainty and pretty, somewhat like a piece of delicate jewelry fashioned from pale green jade. Cone-shaped, with many vertical ridges and cross lines, it is fastened to the leaf by its broad end.

For a couple of days, the egg stays glued to the leaf, showing little outward change except for a gradual darkening. In about seventy-two hours if the weather is warm — slightly longer if it is cool — a tiny head is poked through the shell, and the young caterpillar emerges.

Hardly one-eighth of an inch long, grayish green with a black head, the young future monarch is not much to look at, and, in fact, difficult to spot unless you are searching for it. The tiny fellow comes equipped with

The Caterpillar

all the right instincts, though, the main one being to eat as much and as quickly as possible. For a start, the newly hatched caterpillar thriftily consumes its eggshell and then moves on to feed on the leaf. Being too small and weak at this stage to chew through the entire leaf, it contents itself with eating the soft fleshy parts of the leaf surface, which it does in neat little circles.

After eating all day long for several days, the caterpillar suddenly stops and sits quietly without moving. This does not mean that it has lost its appetite or that it has become tired. Like all other caterpillars, the monarch caterpillar is primarily a simple, efficient, hard-working eating machine. The sudden need to rest means only that the time has come for changing into a larger, more comfortable skin, because the old one is literally bursting at the seams. This happens because the skin of an immature insect does not grow along with the body the way it does in higher animals. Instead, during the entire growth period, the insect's skin has to be shed at intervals to make way for a new, roomier skin that has formed beneath the old one.

A series of contortions starts the actual process of skin-shedding. The caterpillar twists and squirms until the tight old skin splits along the back near the head. Then it thrusts its head through the slit and steps

Enlarged 35 times, the newly hatched monarch caterpillar is shown eating its eggshell (left). Young caterpillars are shown feeding on young milkweed leaves in the illustration at right.

The Caterpillar

out of the old skin, clad in one that is not only brand new but also loose and baggy enough to allow for new growth.

By the time of the first *molt*, as the skin-shedding is called, the caterpillar has almost doubled in length, but even so it is only about a quarter of an inch long. Several additional molts will be necessary before it attains its full size of about two inches.

After the second molt, the body shape and markings of the monarch caterpillar begin to show clearly. In addition to its zebra-like pattern of black-and-white transverse stripes, which presumably serve as a warning to insect-eating animals, it has two pairs of slender, fleshy, black "horns," one pair near the head, the other on the back near the tail end. The pair near the head is the longer of the two. When disturbed, the caterpillar lashes about with these whiplike filaments.

Despite its still small size, the young caterpillar is soon strong enough to cut through the entire milkweed leaf and begin to feed from the edge, cutting out large pieces with amazing speed, efficiency, and untiring energy.

Just about one week after hatching, the caterpillar reaches the halfway mark of its larval stage. It is now almost three-quarters of an inch long and its distinctive pattern of white, yellow, and black stripes is fully defined. The other body features can also be clearly distinguished. They are basically very much the same as in all caterpillars. Typically, butterfly larvae have thirteen body segments, not counting the head. Six true legs are found in pairs on the first three body segments. In addition, however, the caterpillar has five pairs of fleshy, stubby false legs called *prolegs*, one pair each on the third, fourth, fifth, sixth, and last segments of the abdomen. Spiracles, the breathing pores of insects, are located in rows along both sides of the body.

The caterpillar's head comes equipped with strong, short jaws (fine for chewing but useless as weapons), tiny antennae, and simple eyes. With these eyes, the insect can probably do little more than distinguish between light and darkness, but this is quite sufficient for the caterpillar's needs. It does not have to see much to find its food, for the fe-

The Caterpillar

male butterfly always deposits her eggs on her offspring's food plant.

The caterpillar's unique feature is the *spinneret,* the silk-making organ of all moth and butterfly larvae. All caterpillars can produce silk, but the larvae of only certain moth species are regarded as the real silk spinners of commercial importance. The most famous of all, of course, is the silkworm — actually the caterpillar of a rather drab moth originally found in China. This unimportant-looking insect is the one that spins its cocoon of the silk we weave into fine and expensive fabric.

Monarch caterpillars in various growth stages.

The Caterpillar

The spinneret is located at the center of the lower lip. It is a small organ at the opening of the silk glands. Especially while they are young, most caterpillars are dependent upon a strand of silk that forms as they move about. This strand is a kind of guide- and life-line, for it sticks even to a slippery surface, and the caterpillar's feet can cling to it as it moves along. Even if the caterpillar should fall, the strong silken thread keeps the insect attached to its food plant.

During its last larval week, the monarch caterpillar has to more than double its size. The time element may vary with the weather as well as with the individual. If it is very warm, development progresses at a faster rate. For some yet unexplained reason, caterpillars from the same batch of eggs may differ in the time needed to complete the larval stage. Weather cannot be a factor in these cases, and so far no one has offered any other explanation.

As the caterpillar grows, the milkweed food plant clearly shows the effect of its guest's voracious appetite. Many leaves are stripped down to the bare stem, with only the toughest veins remaining intact; others have large pieces cut out of the tender parts. In two weeks of feeding, a single caterpillar may devour as much as four ounces of foliage. Since leaves are as light as they are, this makes quite a pile and highlights the tremendous amount of damage that can be inflicted by caterpillars—chiefly those of certain moth species—that do not feed on weeds, as does the monarch, but on farm crops and other cultivated plants.

The monarch caterpillar's final molt occurs about twelve to fourteen days after hatching. Again, weather has much to do with just when this event takes place. Unseasonably cool temperatures may add as much as two days to the period required for the caterpillar's development.

Finally, however, the moment arrives. The monarch caterpillar prepares for its change into a pupa, the "second act" in the drama of complex metamorphosis.

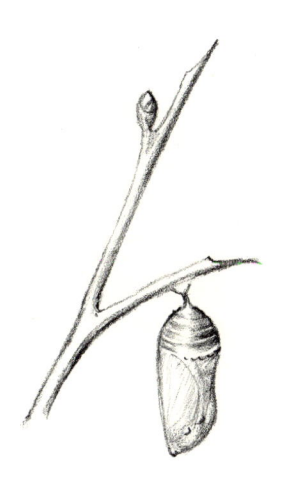

THE CHRYSALIS

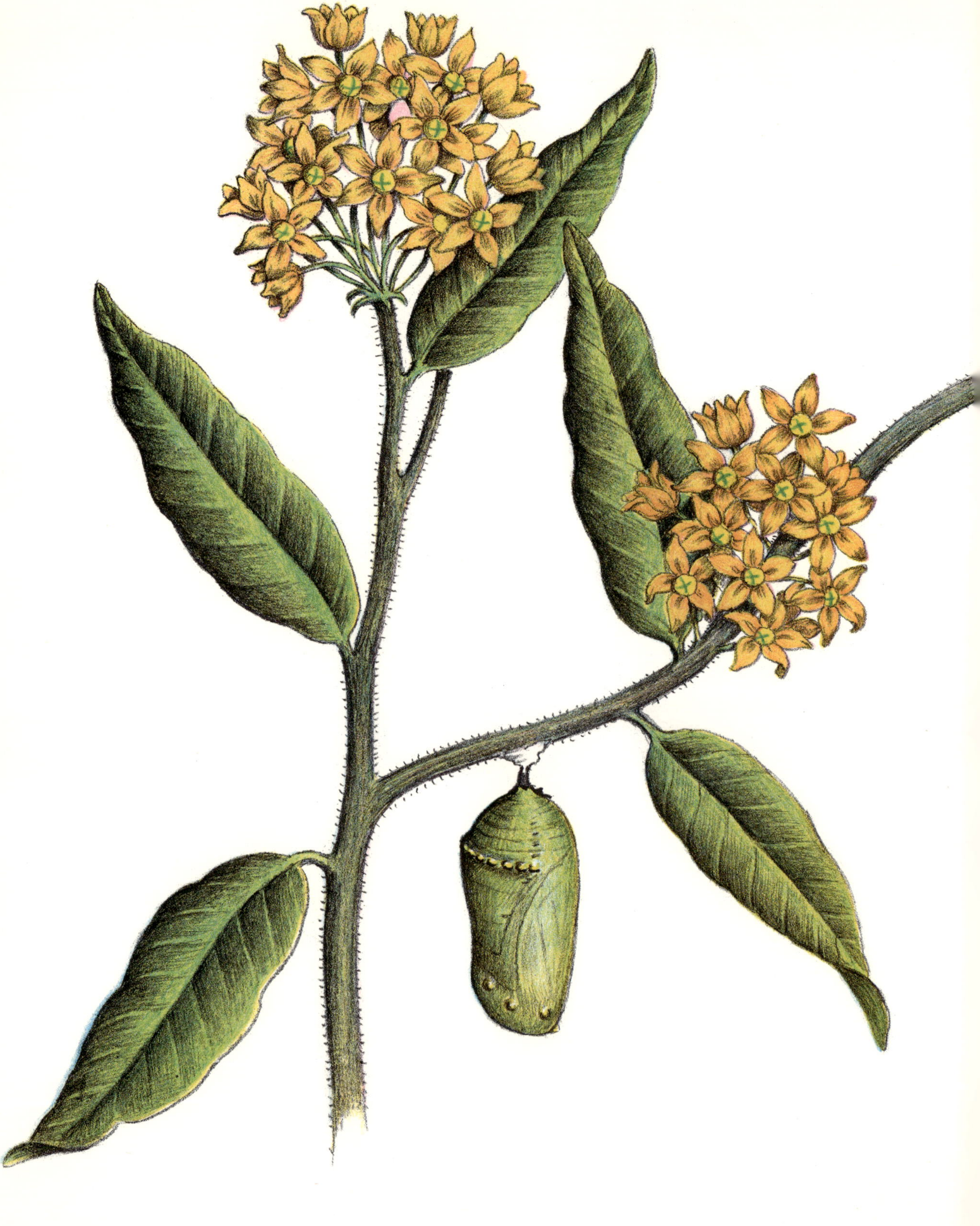

The Chrysalis

The moment the full-grown caterpillar stops eating, it starts the preparations that are necessary for its change into a pupa, or *chrysalis*, as a butterfly pupa is often called. The pupa is a motionless, intermediate stage of the complete metamorphosis, and it distinguishes the most advanced insects from the more primitive kinds. In addition to butterflies and moths, beetles, wasps, bees, ants, and flies undergo a pupal change. Some of these insects, especially those whose larval development takes place underground, do not enclose their pupae in hard shells. All the members of the Lepidoptera protect their pupae in this manner. Thus the changes that take place within the shell during the pupal stage are concealed until the finished product emerges.

Monarch caterpillar hangs suspended from its silken pad shortly before pupating.

Shortly before the last molt, the monarch caterpillar can be seen wandering aimlessly about — or so it appears. Actually, though, it is looking for a suitable spot from which the chrysalis can be suspended. When this has been found, the first step in preparation for the actual change is the spinning of a small silken pad, or carpet. Butterfly larvae do not make cocoons for their pupae, but they do use silk to fasten the chrysalis to a twig, leaf, or whatever other object the caterpillar has chosen as a good place for attaching the pupa.

Completing the pad takes a little while. Moving its head to and fro, the caterpillar adds strand after silken strand until the button-like carpet is the right size. Then it grips this pad with its rearmost pair of prolegs and suspends itself, head down and curved toward the lower surface of its body.

For quite some time it hangs this way without moving. Then, suddenly, a convulsion seems to seize the insect, and after a series of twistings and squirmings, the larval skin splits at the back near the head, bringing into view the green chrysalis shell that has formed underneath. The old skin is now gradually worked toward the tail end. Fi-

The Chrysalis

nally, the pupa withdraws from the skin a short hooked stalk located at the tip of its abdomen, anchors the stalk securely to the silken pad, then drops the old skin altogether, and lets it fall to the ground.

Fully exposed now, fastened to the little pad of silk only by the *cremaster* — the hooked tail end — the chrysalis from this moment on will hang motionless and seemingly lifeless for the next ten days or so. The shell, soft at first, soon begins to harden and assumes a beautiful green color, flecked with what look like specks of real gold. Such gold- and silver-colored chrysalises are typical of many butterflies and explain the term "chrysalis," which comes from the Greek word for "golden."

Hanging immobile by the tip of its tail, the chrysalis remains outwardly unchanged for the next few days. Inside, however, momentous and wonderful changes are taking place. The miraculous chemistry that transforms the caterpillar into a butterfly is in full swing.

After about five days to a week, the originally opaque green color of the chrysalis shell begins to show signs of becoming transparent. An observer can make out, faintly at first, the butterfly wings with their characteristic pattern appearing within the shell. By the time a few

The caterpillar skin is being shed by the newly formed chrysalis.

Monarch chrysalis shortly before emergence of the butterfly. The wings are already visible beneath the shell.

more days have gone by, the green color has disappeared almost completely, and the shell has now taken on the color of smoky glass, beneath which the orange and black colors of the adult monarch's wings are clearly visible.

About ten days after the caterpillar started to spin its little silken carpet, the crucial moment finally approaches for the butterfly to emerge into the world. When that moment arrives, the chrysalis splits along one side, and the monarch slowly works itself out of the shell. After this task is completed, the butterfly, apparently exhausted by its efforts, may cling for a while to the empty shell. Then it usually crawls to the nearest twig or leaf, where it continues to sit and rest quietly.

At this point, the monarch still does not look very much like the big handsome butterfly we are used to seeing in flight. Although the colors and patterns of the wings are all there, the wings are still small and crumpled up like wet paper, and the body looks fat and bloated.

This condition does not last long, however. Even as one watches, the wings spread out and grow larger as the body fluids are pumped into the veins of the wings. At the same time, the body shrinks and takes on its typical, slender shape.

The Chrysalis

Still the monarch continues to sit quietly and wait for the process to finish. The butterfly is very vulnerable at this time, for its wings are too soft to support it in flight, and any damage done to the wings during this period of expansion and drying would cripple the insect for life. However, about one hour after the butterfly has emerged from its shell, the wings have attained their full size and have stiffened sufficiently to be used for flying.

Never again will the monarch be so beautiful as it is at this moment. Its colors are fresh and bright, unmarred, untouched, every scale in place. The black of its body and wings is like velvet, the white spots immaculate, the orange glows with fiery intensity. Later on in its life, the butterfly's wings will show the wear and tear of everyday living, the scars of narrow escapes. Some of the tinted dust will rub off, the colors will appear less bright, and the wings may become frayed and tattered along the edges.

Monarch, moments after having emerged from the pupal shell. Wings are still small and body is bloated by fluids that will be pumped into the wing veins.

The Chrysalis

But now everything is perfect. The waiting period over, the monarch starts to close and open its wings, as if to test whether they are really working properly. At long last, with a flutter, it takes off on its maiden flight, climbing higher and higher into the air that is now its realm. From this hour on, the butterfly will take no food except an occasional sip of nectar as it flits from blossom to blossom, more colorful than many of the flowers it visits.

SUMMER LIFE

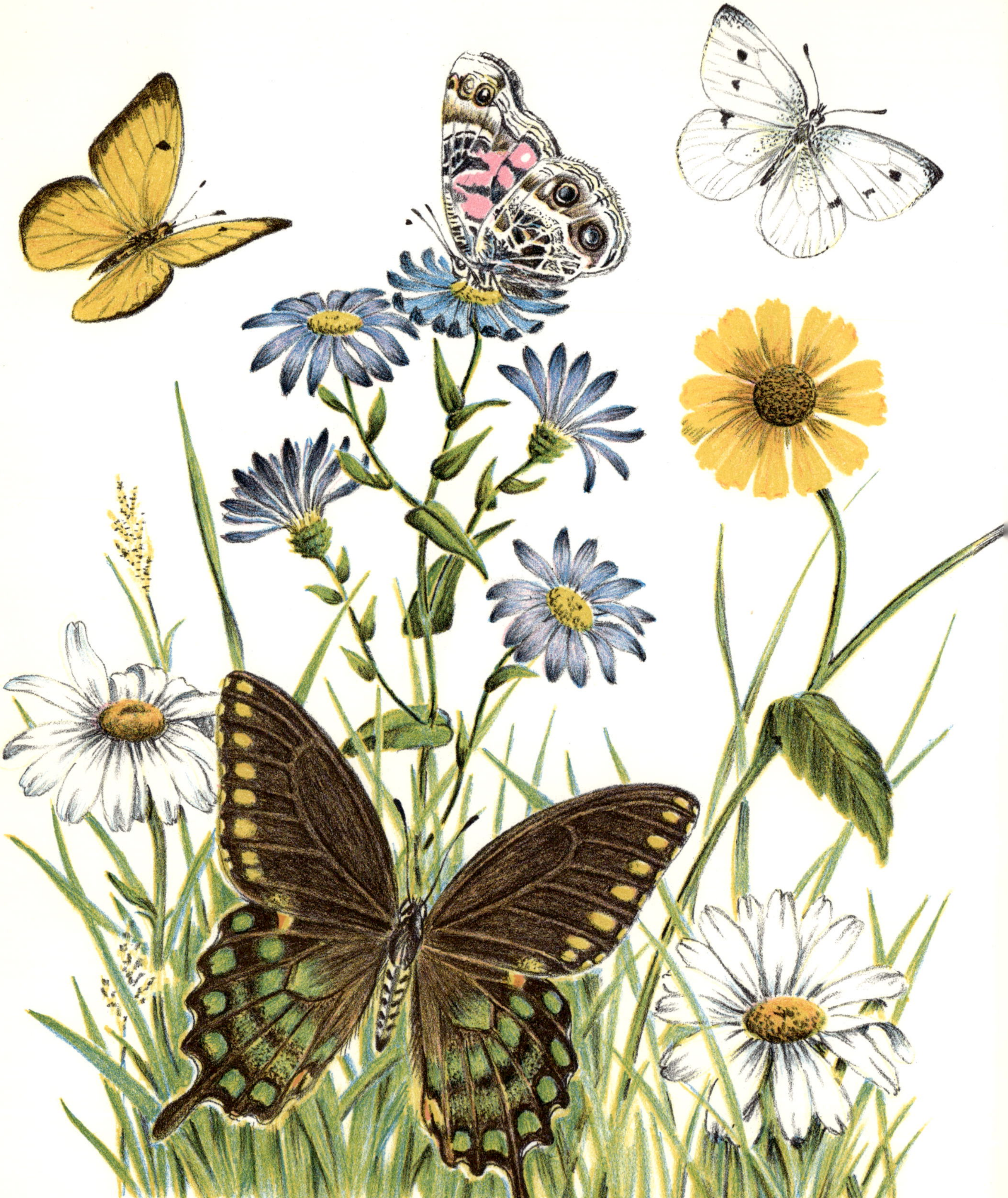

Summer Life

Having taken to the air, the newly emerged monarch now joins others of its tribe in the pursuit of summertime activities. All summer long, from the end of June until September, monarchs can be seen sailing about the meadows, fields, and gardens in many parts of the North American continent. Sometimes they are in the company of other butterflies, more often by themselves, for monarchs will venture into places rarely frequented by most other butterflies. Wherever they appear, though, they are welcome guests.

Secure in their relative immunity from attack by birds, monarchs are not at all shy and are a familiar sight around gardens and houses.

Summer Life

One reason why the monarch has become one of the most widely known of all North American butterflies is that it does not seem to mind being near people.

On close inspection it seems almost impossible to believe that the monarch developed from the white, yellow, and black striped caterpillar, even though we know very well that it did. Every single part of the body and all the colors have changed to such a degree that no particle of resemblance remains. While this is true of all the Lepidoptera, it is especially striking in the case of the large and brightly colored species. In looking at the monarch, we have to remind ourselves that this elegant, slender, black-velvet clad shape adorned by two sets of gleaming orange-and-black wings developed from a fat, wormlike, striped caterpillar. The miracle of metamorphosis strikes us with full force when we consider that little more than a week was needed for the complete transformation of the short-legged, wingless, weak-eyed caterpillar into the winged, long-legged, keen-eyed butterfly.

The praying mantis is a bold and greedy killer. Monarchs and other butterflies frequently fall victim to the well-camouflaged predator.

The monarch has no protection against enemies such as the praying mantis, which is deterred neither by size nor by distasteful body juices.

Although the newly emerged monarch does not have very much to fear from insect-eating birds, this immunity does not hold up for all other enemies. Insect predators especially could not care less that their prey does not taste good to other animals. The praying mantis, for example, is not in the least choosy about its food. This odd-looking killer, a bloodthirsty member of the generally plant-eating group to which grasshoppers and locusts belong, will catch and devour any insect it can get hold of. Well camouflaged by its green or brown coloration, the long-legged menace, its spiked forelegs raised in the typical "praying" position that has given the insect its name, may lurk in any bush or among the flowers visited by butterflies and other nectar-seeking insects.

There are many different species of praying mantids, most of them tropical. North America has three common kinds, two of which were introduced from other parts of the world, one from Europe, and one

Summer Life

from China. The only common native species is the Carolina mantis, the smallest of the three.

For their size, mantids rank as the most voracious and greedy of all insect predators. They will go on killing even while they are busy with the remains of another victim.

Mantids are valued by some farmers and gardeners as destroyers of insect pests. Few people, however, can really warm to their habits. Mantids are cannibals, and not only do parents eat their own offspring if they can catch them, but even the newly hatched young will eat their sisters and brothers if they do not step lively. The female mantis considers the male just the right tidbit for the wedding breakfast, and almost invariably eats him right after mating.

The often-acclaimed value of the mantis as a valuable exterminator of harmful insects is diminished by their indiscriminate slaughter, which includes some of the more valuable pollinators. This becomes clear to anyone who studies the remains of the victims of just a single mantis that has established itself in a flowering bush. Wings and legs of butterflies, honeybees, bumblebees, wasps, and solitary bees can be found on the ground under such a bush. All these insects are important for the fertilization of our fruit-bearing trees, flowers, and other plants.

Monarchs are often among the victims of the praying mantis. Their warning coloration, their distasteful body juices, their rubbery body gives them no protection at all against this killer, which has a completely indiscriminate taste and is not afraid even of such formidable weapons as the poison stings of bees and wasps.

Aside from these hazards, however, the monarch leads a comparatively carefree life during the warm summer months. The butterfly's most important mission, of course, is to find a mate and launch new generations of its species. Male monarchs attract females through an odor sent forth by a small patch of scent scales, visible as small dark spots on one of the veins of the male's hind wings. When a male approaches a female and perfumes the air with his scent, he is making it clear to her that a suitor is at hand and available.

Preliminary to mating, the male monarch (left) perfumes the air around the female with the help of special scent scales, visible as small black patches on the hind wings.

Soon after mating, the female lays her eggs, which in turn will pass through the larval and pupal stages and mature into adult monarchs, all within a month or so. During the span of a single summer, several broods of monarchs complete their metamorphosis, and the ones we see in late summer or early fall may well be the great-grandchildren of those we welcomed in June.

The monarch's life expectancy as an adult is much longer than that of many other butterflies, some of which may live only a few days or weeks at most. The late-summer brood of monarchs, for example, can even expect to live for more than half a year.

Summer Life

Many immature insects, and some adults, including certain butterflies, do not die when cold weather sets in. Instead, they spend the winter *hibernating*, which means that they seek out a suitable hiding place — under bark, a pile of leaves, or in the soil — where they are more or less sheltered. Motionless and in a state where all the normal processes of life, including the metamorphic changes, are suspended, they remain in this shelter until spring once again arrives and warm temperatures bring them back to active life.

Monarchs never hibernate in any stage of their development. Monarch caterpillars or chrysalids that are still around in the fall die when the temperature drops below forty degrees. The adults, however, escape this fate. They have found an alternative to hibernating, an alternative that cannot fail to amaze us in view of the frailty of these insects: they migrate to far-away warm climates. Many of the details of the monarchs' migration still remain a mystery, but even the parts we know make a fascinating story.

MIGRATION

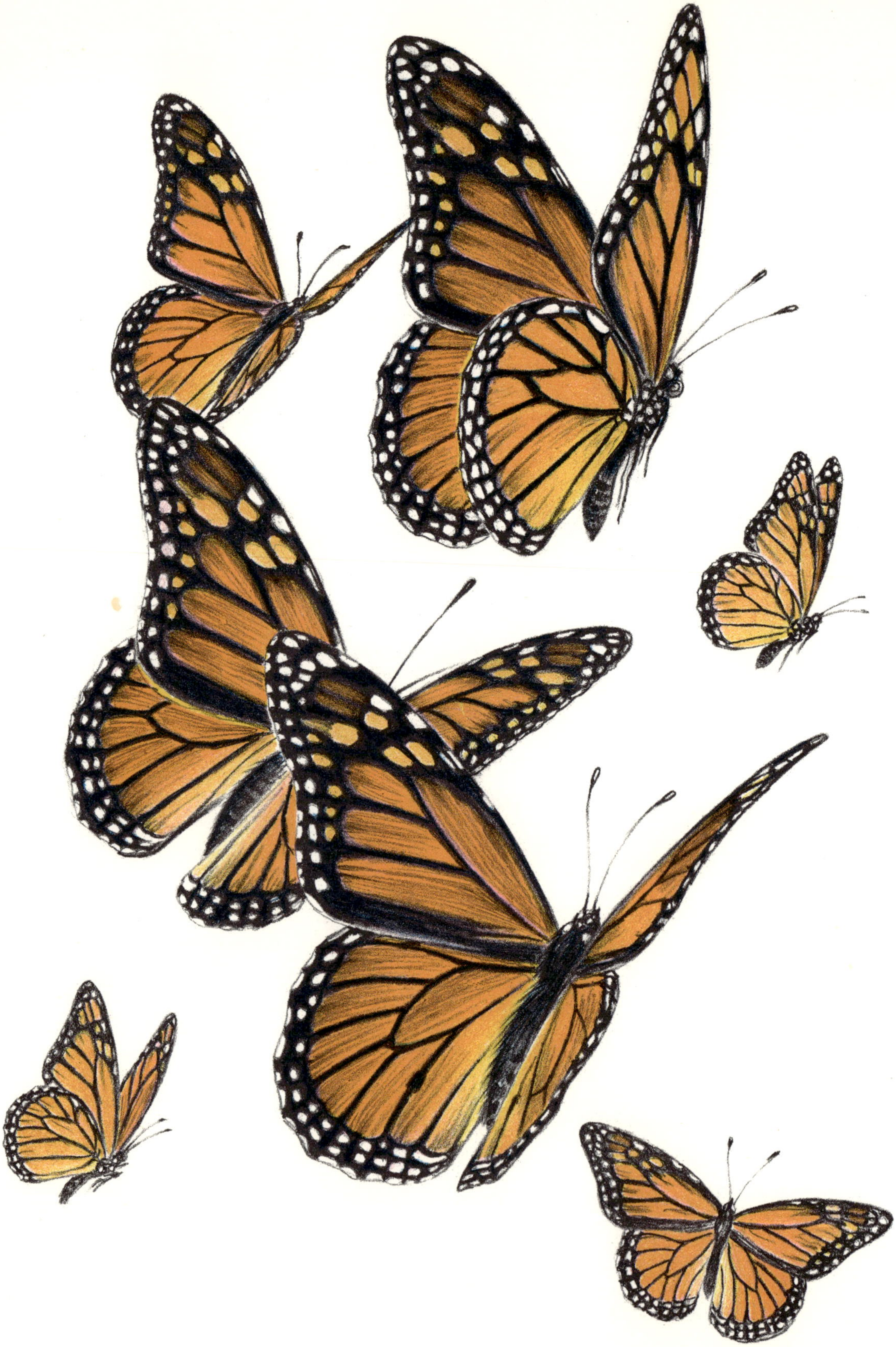

Migration

By far the best-known of all migrations are those made by birds. We are all familiar with such migratory birds as robins, warblers, wild ducks and geese, and others that fly south in the fall, spend the winter in warmer climates, and return again the following spring to their homeland in the north to nest and raise their young.

    Birds are well equipped for such flights. Strong, muscular wings, a special breathing system, a dense and often waterproof body-covering of feathers, the ability to store fat in the tissues, and many other

Migration

physical features make it possible for them to withstand the rigors of long-distance flight. Even so, we cannot help but marvel that small birds often manage to travel thousands of miles during migration.

How much more wonderful and amazing, then, must migrations by butterflies appear to us! Here is the most frail and delicate of creatures, that weighs only a fraction of an ounce, with paper-thin wings, and helplessly exposed to the battering of wind, storm, and rain. It seems almost incredible that such insects should be capable of successfully making journeys of many hundreds and even thousands of miles. Yet some butterflies do just that.

One of the most famous of the migratory butterflies is the European thistle butterfly, commonly known as the painted lady. It is a comparatively small butterfly with a wingspread of about two inches. But its small size has not kept it from being probably the most adventurous — and accordingly the most widely distributed — member of its entire order. North Africa was presumably the original home of this butterfly, but it is now found all over Europe and in many other parts of the world. From time to time, large flocks of these butterflies can be seen crossing the Mediterranean on their way from Africa to Europe. These migrations are not seasonal and have nothing to do with any attempt to seek out better climates. Instead, they seem to be the result of periodic "population explosions" among these butterflies.

Although few insects will attempt to cross large bodies of water, painted ladies have been sighted flying along, hundreds of miles out over the ocean. Their distribution thus appears to be due largely to their own efforts, and not, as in the case of so many other insects, to accidental transportation of larvae or adults through man.

The painted lady may be the most widely spread migratory butterfly, but the monarch is more famous because it is the only butterfly known to make *seasonal* migrations, much in the manner of birds. At one time this seemed so incredible that it was doubted until recently. And the more facts we learn about the long-distance travels of the monarch, the more amazing they appear.

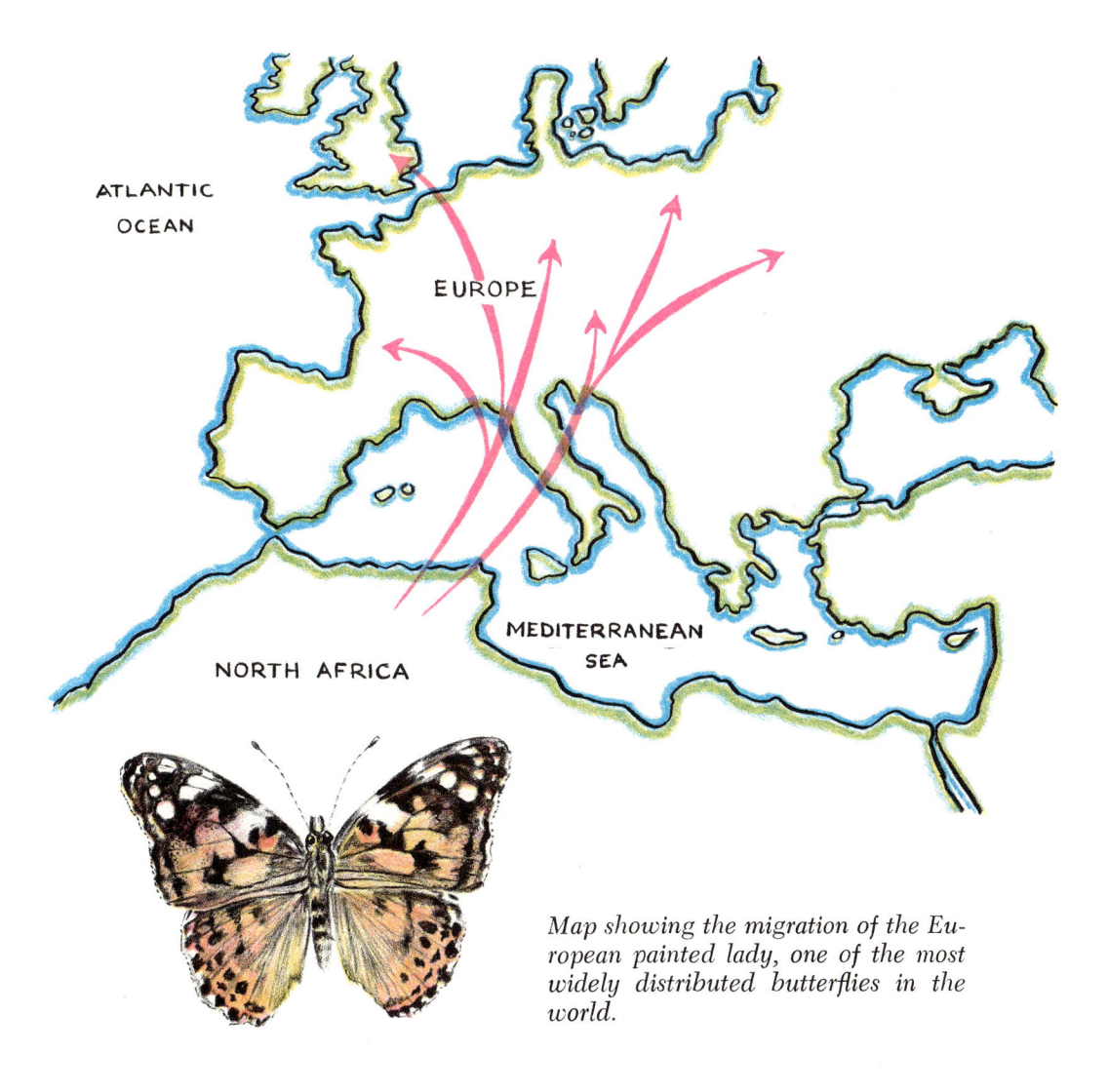

Map showing the migration of the European painted lady, one of the most widely distributed butterflies in the world.

Although many details are still unknown, naturalists have pieced together enough data on the monarch migrations to clear up any lingering doubts that these mass flights to winter quarters do, indeed, take place every year.

The story of the migration begins when autumn brings cool weather to the more northern regions of our continent. At that time, usually in September, monarchs start to gather, first in small groups, then in throngs much in the manner of swallows and other birds flocking together for their fall migrations.

The swarm takes off in a southerly direction, growing in size as

Monarchs gathering in small groups preparatory to their seasonal fall migration.

other monarchs join along the way. Some of these swarms may eventually number in the thousands, or even tens of thousands. Flying by day, the butterflies rest at night, often settling in great numbers in certain trees, like roosting birds. These trees are sometimes covered so densely with resting monarchs that the foliage can hardly be seen under the mass of orange-and-black wings. One of the most interesting facts about the resting places of these butterflies is that, year after year, successive swarms will select not only the same kind of tree, but actually the same trees picked as roosting places by those monarchs that passed that way in earlier years.

When morning arrives and the first rays of the sun warm the butterflies' wings, the crowd stirs, and soon the monarchs are off again on their long journey southward.

The greatest concentration of these migratory swarms usually appears along the eastern and western seaboards of the United States. They may also occur in other parts of the country, although perhaps not in such large numbers. Huge flocks of monarchs have been observed flying over New York City during fall migration time.

Many swarms stop when they reach the Gulf states and central and southern California. Others, however, continue on to subtropical regions, sometimes even crossing wide stretches of open water. The fact that monarchs have been seen flying far out over the ocean has set some scientists wondering whether, at least occasionally, these adventurous butterflies, aided by a tail wind, may not have succeeded in actually crossing entire oceans under their own power.

Bird migrations have been studied extensively, especially within the last few decades. Bird banding — the marking of birds by placing small metal rings around their legs — has been used successfully as a means of tracking their flights. With the cooperation of naturalists in many lands, the migratory travels of a number of different kinds of birds have been recorded rather accurately, and we now have considerable knowledge about where, how fast, and how far these birds journey during their migrations.

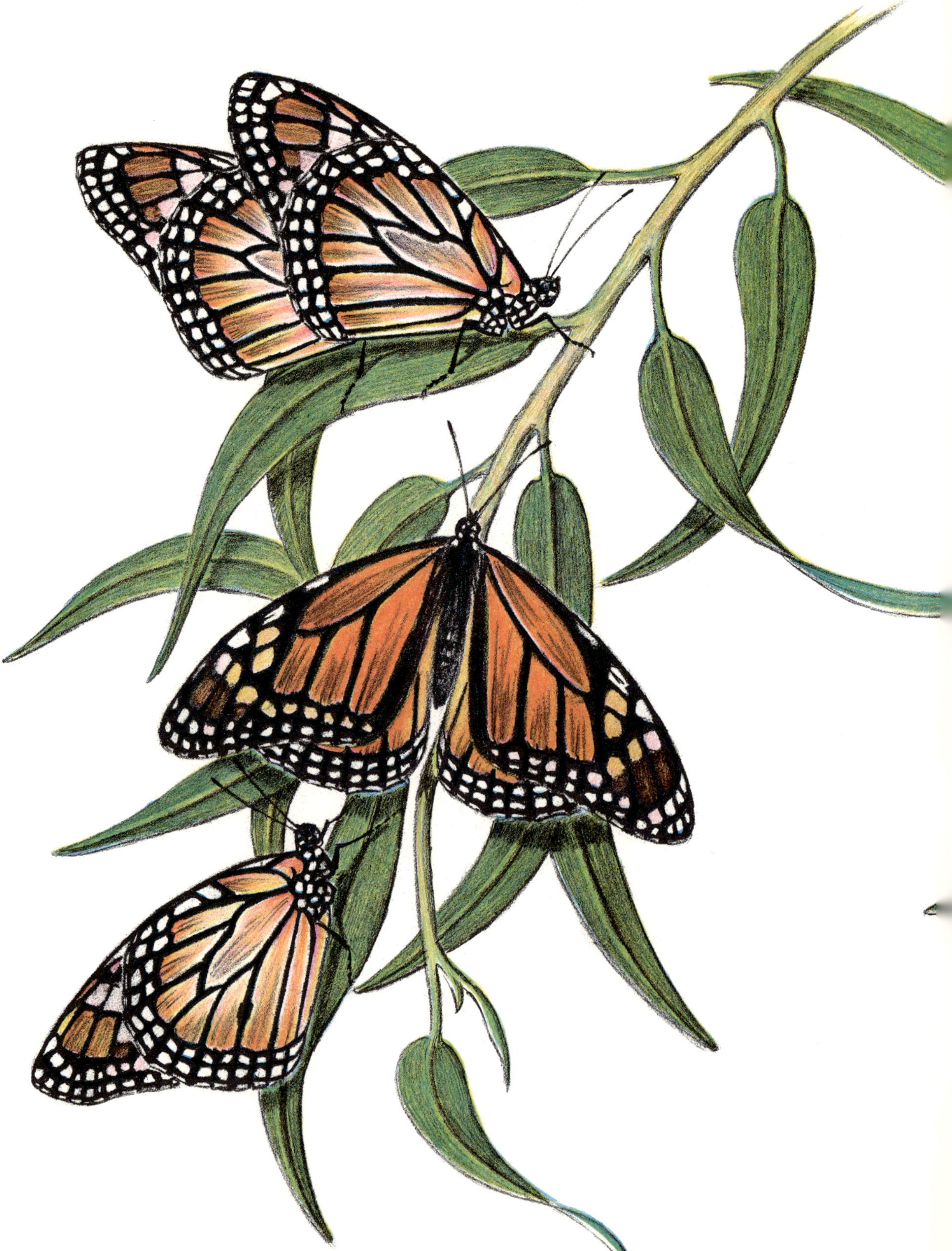

In their winter quarters, monarchs gather in great masses in certain trees. In California, the "monarch trees" are rigorously protected by local laws.

For obvious reasons, butterfly banding is a difficult undertaking. Attempts to mark certain monarchs in a way that would enable zoologists to recognize and identify them easily — by attaching small bits of paper to their hind wings, for instance — have been made, but these attempts have not been too successful, and the findings gathered in this way not conclusive. A new safe, foolproof device for clearly marking butterflies without disabling or hurting them is still to be discovered. If and when such a method is invented, a lot more may be learned about the details of the monarch's migration.

Even though our present knowledge remains spotty and incomplete, we do have a good deal of information about the life of our butterflies in their winter quarters. In California especially they have been closely observed and studied. The small town of Pacific Grove, some sixty miles south of San Francisco, is almost as famous for the annual visits of the monarchs as San Juan Capistrano in the south is for the punctual annual return of its faithful swallows. In Pacific Grove, the big butterflies turn up at about the same time each year and settle in large numbers on the same trees used by the swarms of the year before.

During their stay in winter quarters, monarchs usually are not very active. They do not fly about as much as they did during the summer, and they stay more or less together. The fascinating spectacle of thousands of these butterflies clinging to "their" trees is one of the major attractions in Pacific Grove, which proudly calls itself "Butterfly Town, USA." The strictest legal protection of the beautiful winter guests is enforced in every part of California where the migratory swarms appear. In Pacific Grove, anyone caught hurting or molesting the monarchs in any way — throwing a stone at one of the "butterfly trees," for example — is punishable by a five-hundred-dollar fine. In addition, he exposes himself to the wrath of a population that loves its monarchs and anxiously watches over their welfare.

When spring arrives and the weather in the northern parts of our continent starts to warm up, the monarchs' wonderful instinct lets them

Female monarch laying eggs on milkweed. The old females usually die shortly after the eggs have been deposited.

know that the time has come for the return trip. The northbound migration, however, is by no means as massive and concentrated a movement as the fall migration. Instead, the butterflies straggle north in small groups, with the females stopping along the way to lay their eggs on various kinds of milkweed plants. The old, tired females then die. It must be assumed that very few, if any, of the individuals that survived the winter reach the place from which they started their southward journey in the previous fall.

The monarchs that eventually develop from these eggs, however,

Map showing migration routes of both the Atlantic and Pacific monarch populations. Red arrows show the massive southward fall migration, blue arrows the rather straggling northbound flights. Winter quarters in California and the Gulf regions are indicated.

Atlantic Ocean

Gulf of Mexico

South America

Migration

instinctively continue to fly north. Some of the offspring travel far up into Canada, where they mate, lay their eggs, and die. Then, one day the next fall, the time again comes for new generations of monarchs to follow their migratory instincts and leave the northern regions before the cold weather kills them. Gathering in flocks, they will wing their way south to their winter havens, as others of their kind have done year after year in the past, so that their kind may continue to survive and flourish.

RAISING MONARCHS AT HOME

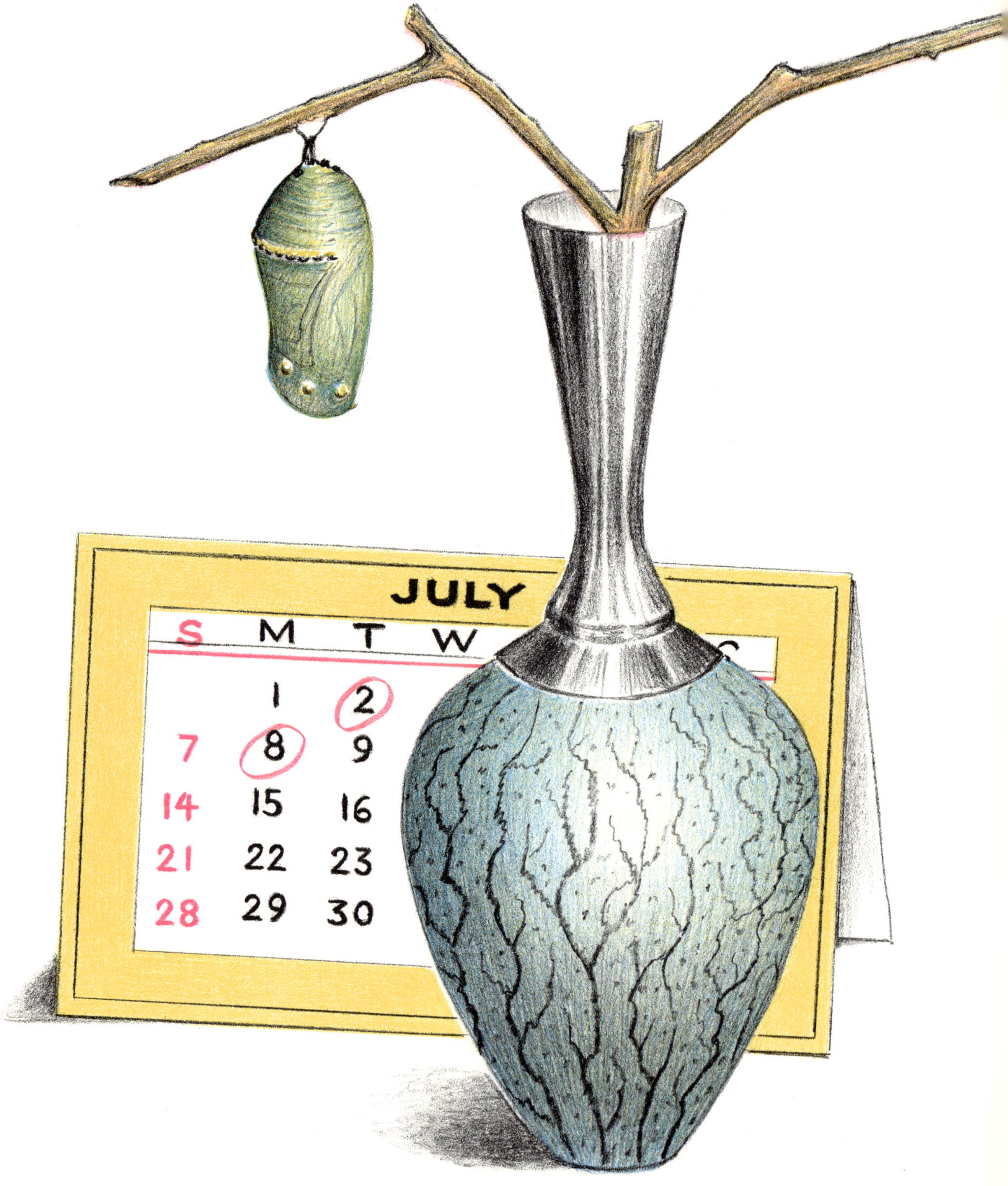
JULY
S M T W
1 2
7 8 9
14 15 16
21 22 23
28 29 30

Raising Monarchs at Home

No amount of reading about a butterfly's metamorphosis can compare with watching this miracle yourself. Raising butterflies in your home becomes difficult only if the food plant for any particular species is hard to obtain, for just a few simple rules have to be observed to make sure the caterpillar will successfully complete its transformation. Anybody willing to do this, and who lives near fields, meadows, or even empty lots in various parts of North America, should have no difficulty at all in successfully raising monarchs at home. Milkweed is a common plant, and is easily found in abundance.

The care of the caterpillar demands little effort and attention. And what a thrill it is to watch the small larva grow, shed its skin, change into a pupa, and then, finally, to see the butterfly emerge from its shell in all its virginal perfection!

The first thing to do is to find the right plants and examine them for eggs and caterpillars. Several species of milkweed grow in various parts of the United States. They grow to be several feet high and they have rather stiff, straight stems, long, narrow leaves, and clusters of small pinkish or orange blossoms.

After locating the plants, look for leaves with large semi-circular pieces missing — usually a sign that monarch caterpillars have been at work. It is easy to see the half-grown caterpillars with their distinctive white-yellow-black markings. It is more interesting, however, to pick up eggs or very small larvae, and to watch the process from the very start. But eggs are not so easy to find, and you may have to content yourself with the half-grown caterpillars.

Milkweed plants with eggs or larvae on the leaves should be cut carefully in order not to dislodge the insects or hurt them. Even a slight pressure will squash their soft bodies.

You can keep your caterpillars in almost any kind of container which will admit light and air. A large Mason jar or, even better, an old discarded fish tank will serve this purpose. Cover the bottom with gravel or leaf mold. Fill a small bottle or plastic container with water, bury it up to its neck in the gravel, and place the cut end of your milkweed into it. The plant will stay fresh much longer this way. Cover the top of the jar with cheesecloth.

Now you can watch your caterpillars. Remember to replace wilted plants with fresh ones from time to time, for caterpillars require a steady supply of food. When you replace the plants, be careful to transfer the caterpillars without squeezing them. Unnecessary handling should be avoided in any case.

Although the caterpillars should have light, never place the container where it will remain in direct sunlight. The larvae are sensitive

Raising Monarchs at Home

to extreme temperatures, and too much heat may easily kill them.

When the caterpillars approach the stage of full growth, it is advisable to put a sturdy twig into the container. This gives the insects a secure place to which they can fasten the silk pad from which the pupa will be suspended.

If at all possible, try to observe the process that transforms the caterpillar into the chrysalis. It is a fascinating performance, but you will have to be patient, because it may take many hours before the last molt is completed and the pupal shell appears. If you are lucky enough to find a number of caterpillars in the same growth stage, or if you can raise them from the eggs, chances are that some of them will pupate at about the same time. If your luck holds, you may enjoy the breathtaking experience of seeing, within the span of a few minutes, several

A common species of North American milkweed, with flowers and seed cases. Monarch caterpillars feed on this and other milkweed species.

Raising Monarchs at Home

monarchs emerge from their chrysalises and start to expand their immaculate wings. Without a doubt, this is one of nature's most fascinating and dramatic spectacles. One naturalist, even after a long and eventful life, regarded as one of the most memorable of all his experiences the day he, as a ten-year-old-boy, watched more than two hundred European peacock butterflies break open their chrysalis shells and emerge.

When your monarchs start to emerge, be sure not to touch or otherwise disturb them. Also, they have to have enough room to spread their wings without meeting any obstacle. (If your container is small, remove the twig with the pupa and put it in a vase — the pupa will stay where it is. Just make sure that it hangs freely.) Any damage done to the wings in the early stages, before they have had a chance to fully spread and harden, will cripple the butterfly for life and destroy its ability to fly.

As the wings expand, watch to see how the body grows more slender minute by minute as the body fluids are pumped into the wing veins, until the wings finally reach their full four-inch span.

After expansion and hardening of the wings is completed — which takes about an hour from the time the butterfly breaks from its shell — you may, if you wish, try to feed your monarch its first meal. Moisten a finger with water into which a little sugar has been dissolved. Then gently push the finger underneath the butterfly's head. The insect may decide to climb onto a proffered finger without the slightest hesitation, and, once its sensitive feet "taste" the sugar, it may readily uncoil its long sucking tube and lap up some of the sweet liquid.

Butterflies never should be held captive for long. They are creatures of freedom, open air, and sun. Indeed, they will beat their wings against the confining walls of any cage or window panes until their scales rub off and the once-beautiful color patterns are ruined. The best and kindest thing is to set them free, thereby giving them the chance to enjoy the summer days and propagate their kind.

Take your monarch to an open window. It may be content to sit quietly for a little while, opening and closing its wings. Then suddenly,

Raising Monarchs at Home

with a flutter, it will be gone, soaring out and up into the sky. If your monarch happens to be one that has emerged late in summer, it may well live to travel hundreds or even thousands of miles, spend the winter in warmer climates, and then turn north again to start new generations of regally handsome orange-and-black butterflies.

APPENDIX

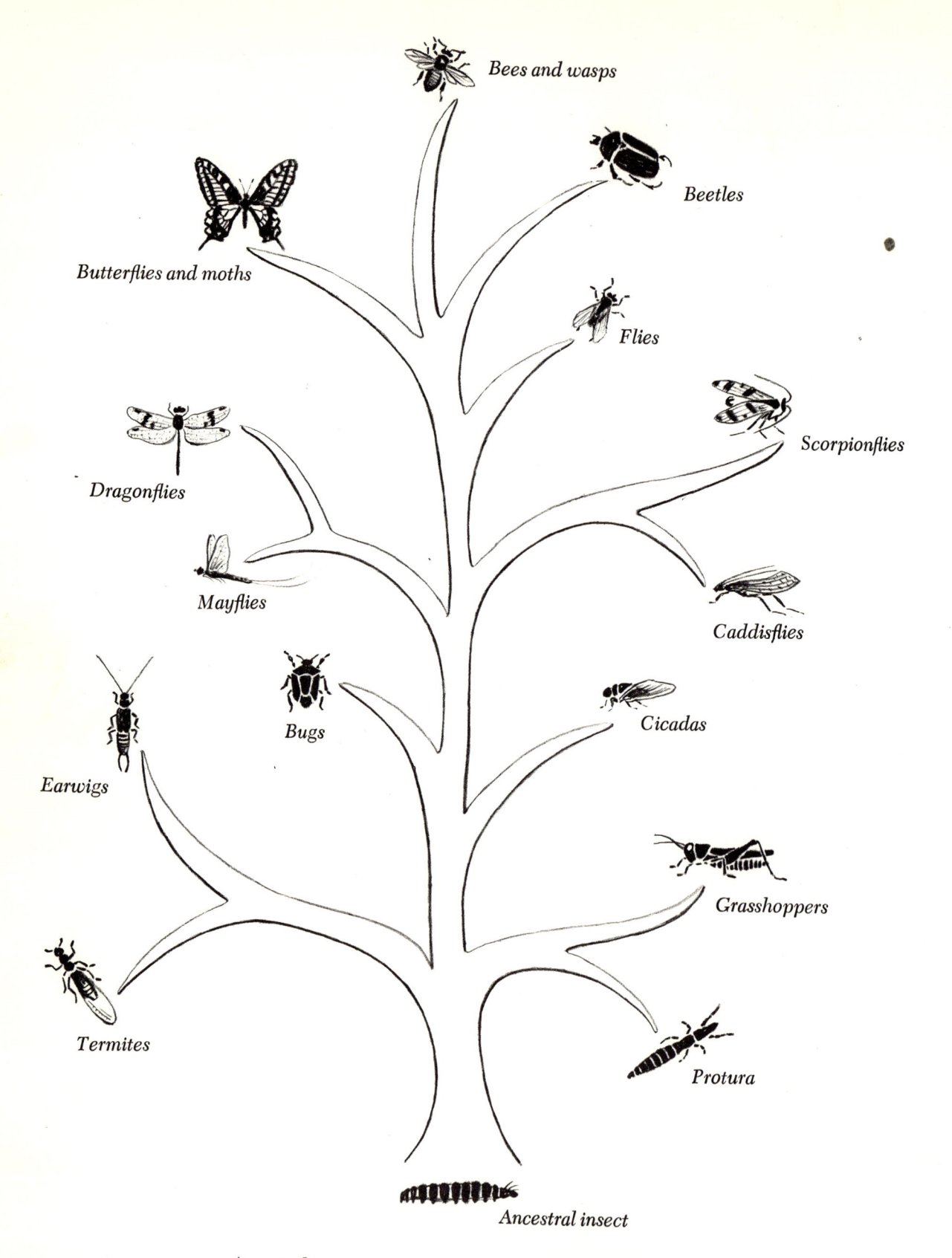

Ancestral tree of the insects, starting with the most primitive and branching out into the more advanced members.

DIRECT DEVELOPMENT (silverfish)

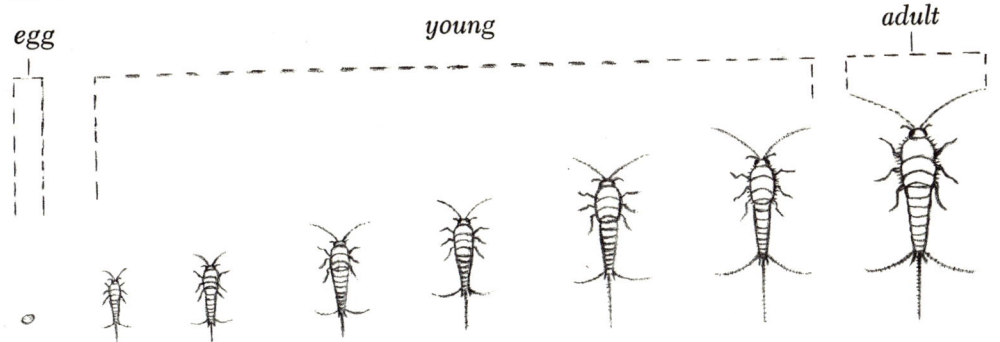

The most primitive insects have a direct development. The young resemble the adults in all details.

GRADUAL DEVELOPMENT (bug)

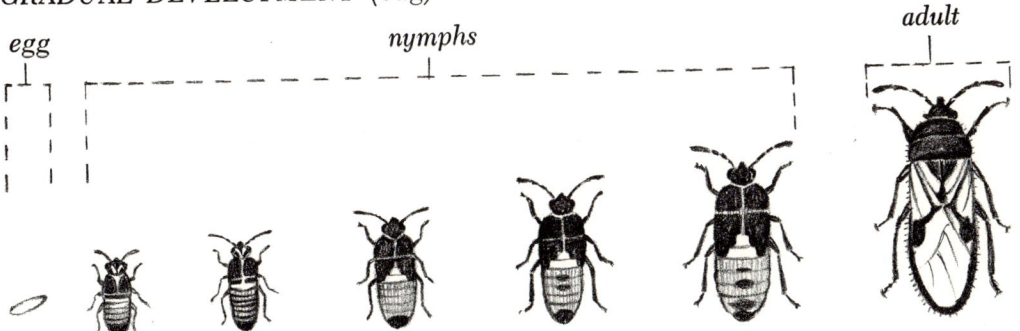

The "gradual" development, or incomplete metamorphosis, is found in the more advanced insects. The young, called nymphs, lack certain adult features — functional wings, for example.

COMPLEX DEVELOPMENT (butterfly)

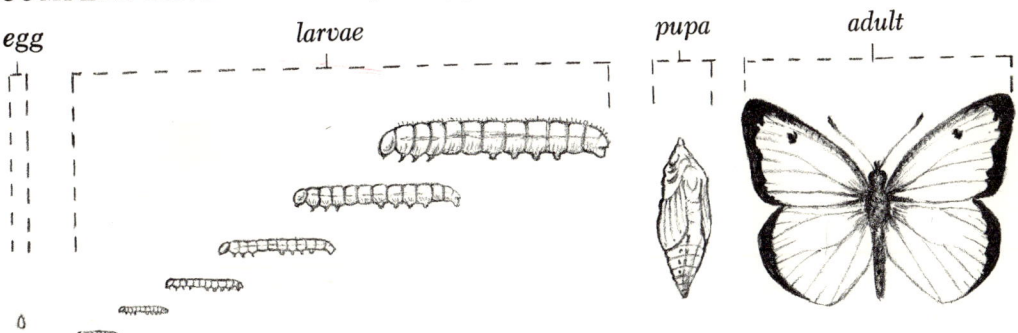

Complex development, or complete metamorphosis, is a feature of the most advanced insects. It involves four stages: egg, larva, pupa, and adult. The immature young do not resemble the adults.

Various forms of development among insects.

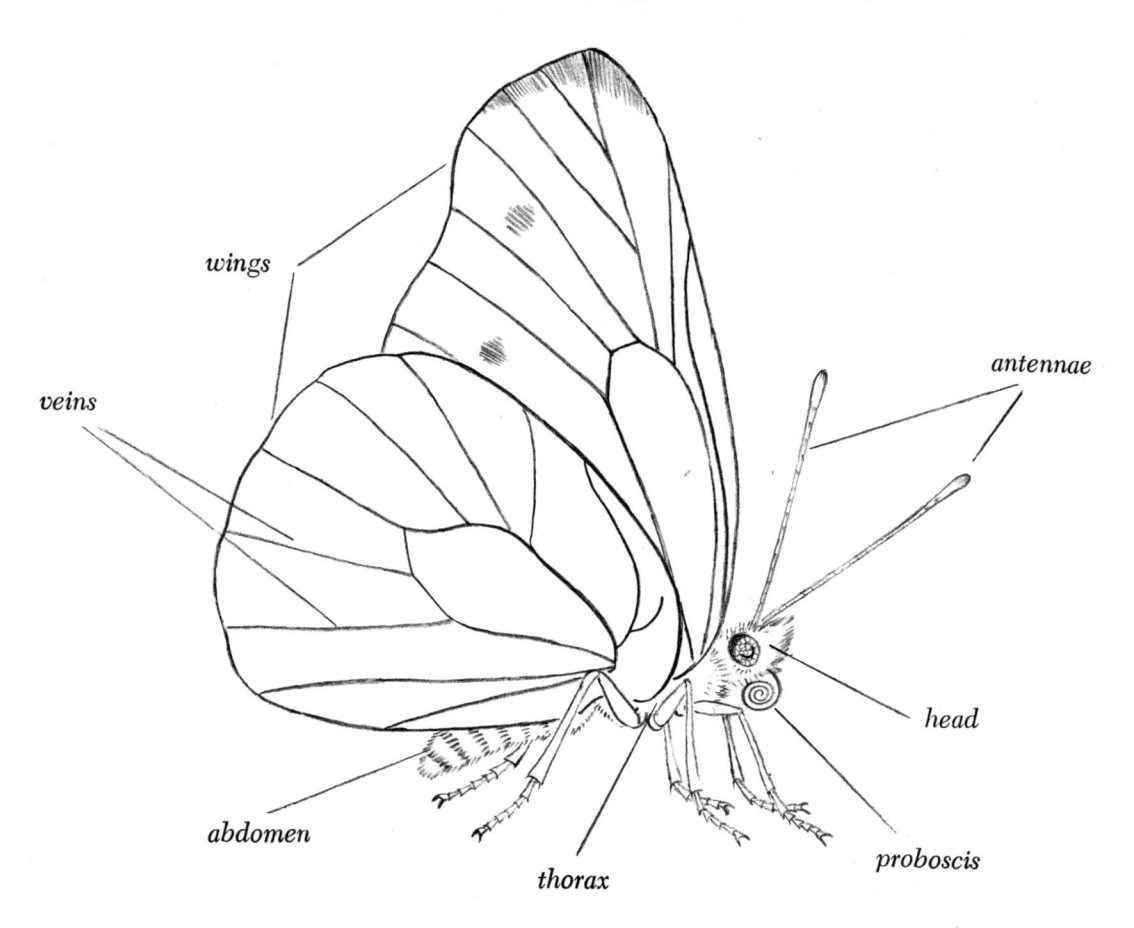

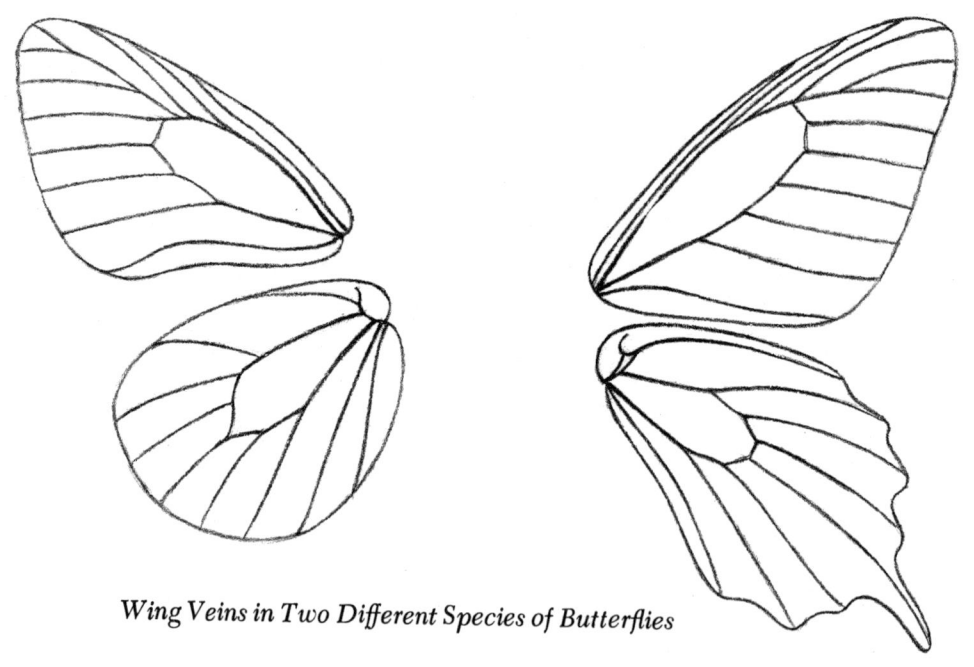

Diagram Showing Parts of a Butterfly

Wing Veins in Two Different Species of Butterflies

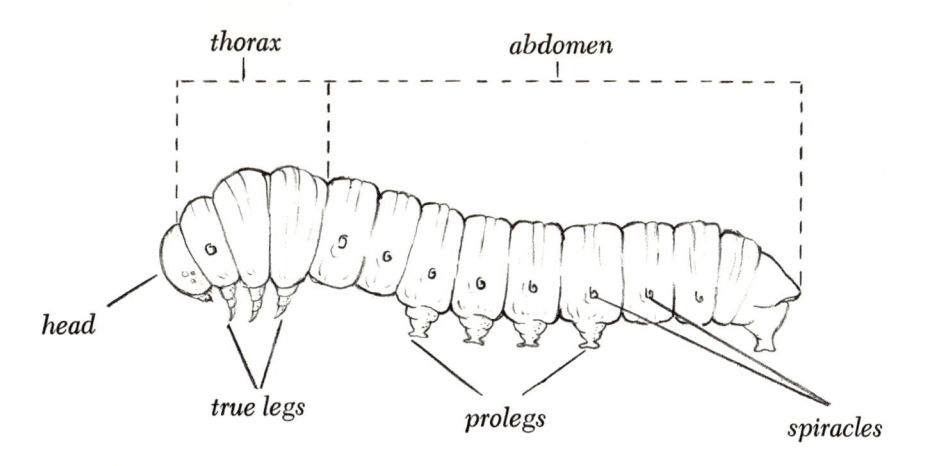

Diagram Showing Parts of a Caterpillar

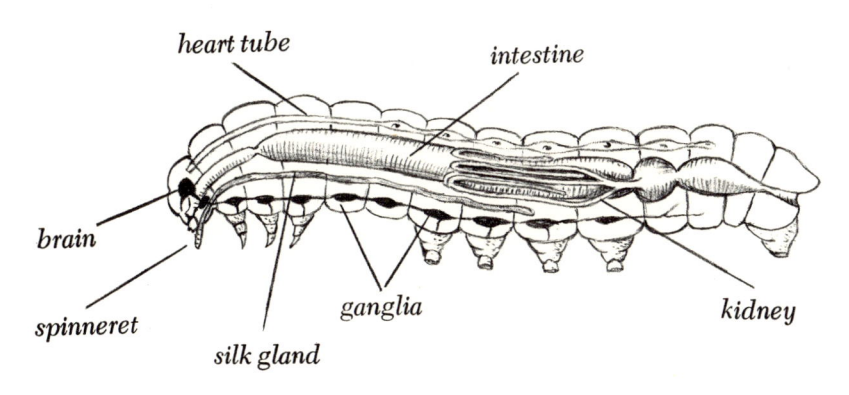

Internal Parts of a Caterpillar (simplified)

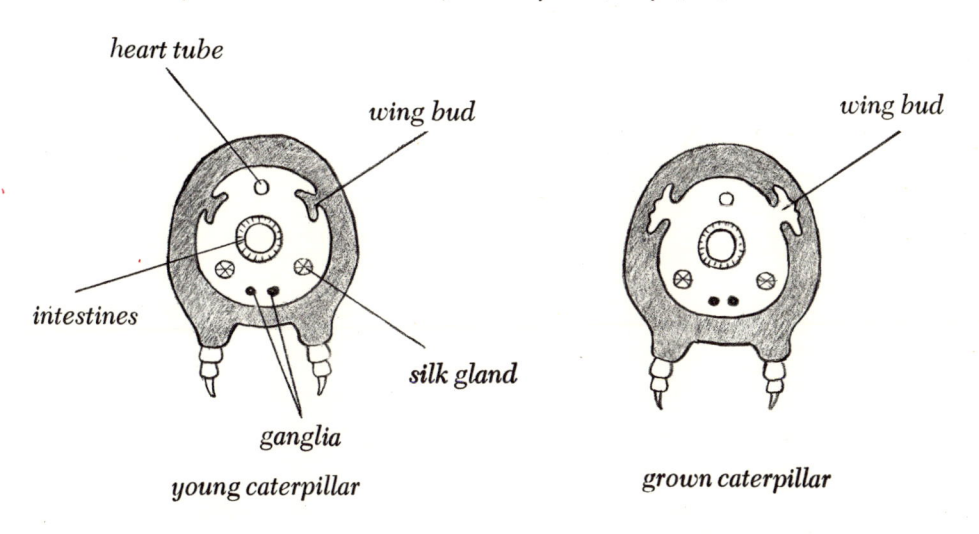

young caterpillar   grown caterpillar

Transverse Cut Through a Caterpillar's Body

113

Glossary of Zoological Terms Used in This Book

Ab-do′men — The posterior section of the body, behind the thorax, in insects and crustaceans. The abdomen is made up of segments whose number differs in the various species. As a rule, no insect has more than 11 abdominal segments even in the immature stage, and fewer in the adult.

Ad-vanced′ — In zoology, a term used for animal groups whose anatomical structure, development, or both, have become more complex than that of their *primitive* relatives.

An-ten′nae (sing. An-ten′na) — Movable, segmented organs of sensation on the heads of insects and certain other animals, including crustaceans. Popularly called *feelers* or *horns*.

Cam′ou-flage — In zoology, body pattern and coloring of an animal that tends to let the animal blend in with its background and thus hide it from enemy eyes; a deceptive disguise that makes an animal inconspicuous.

Chrys′a-lis — The pupa of certain insects, especially butterflies. The word is of Greek derivation, from *chrysos,* gold. Many butterfly chrysalises have gold-and-silver-colored or -flecked shells.

Class — A comprehensive group of animals which, in zoological classification, ranks above an order. Thus mammals, birds, and insects are examples of animal classes. Each class has a number of *orders*, which are subdivided into *families*. Families are made up of several *genera* (sing. genus), and the genera, in turn, usually of a number of *species*.

Co-coon′ — The envelope, often made of silk, which the larvae of many insects form about themselves as they pass into the pupal stage. The pupa remains in the cocoon until the adult insect is ready to emerge.

Zoological Terms

Cre-ma′ster	A short hooked stalk at the end of the abdomen with which certain caterpillars attach themselves to a silken pad shortly before transformation into a pupa.
Di-mor′phism	Difference in form, color, or structure between members of the same species; in zoology especially, unusual differences such as having two forms or color phases in the same species.
Fam′i-ly	A group of related animals forming a category that is above the *genus* and below the *order*. All the scientific family names of animals end in "idae," as, for example, *Danaidae*, the milkweed butterflies.
Ge′nus	A group of related species; in classification, a category ranking between the species and the family. The genus name is the first part of an animal's scientific name, and is always capitalized, as, for instance, *Danaus chrysippus*.
Hi′ber-nate	To pass the winter in a lethargic state, where all activity is either much reduced or stopped altogether, and little or no food is consumed.
Lar′va	The immature, wingless, and often worm-like form, the second stage of *complete metamorphosis*, in which the young of *advanced* insects remain until time comes to pupate. The larvae of various insect species may be known as *grubs*, *maggots*, or *caterpillars*.
Met-a-mor′pho-sis	A marked and usually rather abrupt change in form and structure, and usually also in way of life, food, etc.
Mim′ic-ry	In the strict zoological sense, a superficial resemblance of certain animals, especially insects, to other, often unrelated species, through which the *mimic* gains some protection.
Mod′el	An animal, usually an insect, that has a natural protection either through weapons such as poison stings, or through distasteful or poisonous body juices, and is *mimicked* by unprotected species.

Zoological Terms

Molt
: To shed or cast off hair, feathers, outer layers of skin, etc., at certain times when the cast-off parts are replaced with new growth. Among insects, only the immature young molt, never the adults.

Or'der
: A category ranking below a class and above a family.

Pro-bos'cis
: Any of various tubular elongations of the heads of animals; the snout; in insects the word is usually used for the tubular sucking organ.

Pro'leg
: One of the fleshy, stubby legs found on the abdominal segments of the larvae of certain insects such as moths and butterflies.

Pro-tec'ted
: In zoology, a term often used for animals, especially insects, which have defensive devices such as poison stings, foul odors or secretions, or evil-tasting body juices. Such insects often serve as *models* for unprotected species.

Pu'pa
: The third stage of complete metamorphosis; an intermediate and usually quiescent form found in the *advanced* insects. Butterfly pupae are often called *chrysalises*.

Spe'cies
: The basic category of classification; a group of animals, below the genus, that possess one or more distinctive characters in common, and that can and do interbreed and reproduce their distinctive features in their offspring. The second portion of an animal's scientific name, always spelled in lower case, is the species name, as in *Danaus chrysippus*, a milkweed butterfly of the genus *Danaus*, the species *chrysippus*.

Spin'ner-et
: An organ for producing a thread of silk from the secretion of the silk glands in spiders and most caterpillars.

Spi'ra-cle
: A breathing hole; an external opening of the trachea in insects and terrestrial arthropods, placed along the sides of the thorax and abdomen.

Tho'r-ax
: The middle section of an insect's body, bearing a pair of legs on each of its three segments.

Tra'che-a
: One of the air tubes that form the breathing system of insects and certain other animals.

Index

Advanced, definition of zoological term, 114
   insects, *see* Insects, advanced
African monarch, 33, 34, 50, 51; *ill.*, 30, 52 *(see also Danaus chrysippus)*
   caterpillar, 34; *ill.*, 33
Amauris, 34, 36, 50
Antennae, 18 *(see also* Feelers)
Asclepiadaceae, 23 *(see also* Asclepias plants)
Asclepias plants, 28, 58 *(see also* Milkweed)

Bates, Henry W., 48, 49, 50, 51
Blues, *ill.*, 16-17
Bumblebee, *see* Insect, "models"
Butterflies, 15-17, 22; *ill.*, 14-15 *(see also* Milkweed, butterflies)
   abdomen, 17, 18; *ill.*, 112
   anatomy, 17-18; *ill.*, 112
   antennae, 18; *ill.*, 112
   behavior, 24
   blue, *ill.*, 16-17
   body structure, 17
   cabbage, 49
   caterpillar, 17; *ill.*, 113
   colors, 19-20
   compound eye, 18
   development, 17; *ill.*, 111
   economic importance, 17
   food, 17, 18
   instinct, 24, 95
   larva, 17
   metamorphosis, 17; *ill.*, 111
   peacock, 106
   population, 16, 59
   pupa, 17
   scales, 19-23; *ill.*, 21-23
   sense of taste, 19
   swallowtail, 50, 51, 58
   thistle, 90; *ill.*, 91
   thorax, 17; *ill.*, 112
   white, 49
   wings, 17; *ill.*, 112
Butterfly, cabbage, 49
"Butterfly Town, USA," 96
Butterfly trees, 96
"Butterfly weed," *see* Milkweed

Cabbage butterfly, 49
Camouflage, 44, 114; *ill.*, 44
Caterpillar, 17 *(see also* Larva, Monarch, caterpillar)
   African monarch, 34; *ill.*, 33
   anatomy, *ill.*, 113
   body features, 68
   North American monarch, 65-70; *ill.*, 64-65, 67, 69
Chrysalis, 73, 76 *(see also* Pupa)
   colors, 75
   definition, 114
Churchill, Sir Winston, 16
Class, definition, 114
Cocoon, 69, 74
   definition, 114
Color of butterflies, 19-23
   camouflage, 24
   iridescent, 22
   pigmental, 20, 21
   structural, 20, 21
   warning, 23
Compound eye, 18
Cremaster, 75
   definition, 114

Index

Danaida, 36
Danaidae, *see* Danaids
Danaids, 23, 24, 32, 34, 37, 51
    (*see also* Milkweed butterflies)
  African, 33, 34
  behavior, 24
  caterpillars, 24
  Central American, 26, 27, 40; *ill.*, 38-39
  colors, 23
  Indo-Australian, 35
  North American, 57-62
  tropical, 28; *ill.*, 26-27
  South American, 36-37, 40, 54; *ill.*, 38-39
Danaus chrysippus, 33, 50; *ill.*, 32
  chrysippus alcippus, 33; *ill.*, 32
  chrysippus dorippus, 33
  leonippus indicus, 35
  schenkii periphas, 35
  tytia nephonica, 35
Darwin, Charles, 36-48, 51
Diffusion, *see* Light, diffusion
Dimorphism, 50
  definition, 115

Economic importance of insects, *see* Insects
Electron microscope, 21
Euploea, 36; *ill.*, 36
Evolution, theory of, 46

Family, definition of zoological term, 115
Feelers, 18 (*see also* Antennae)

Genus, definition of zoological term, 115
Golden Danaid, 33, 34

Heliconiids, 37
Hibernation of insect, 86
Hornets, *see* Insect, "models"
Hypolimnas misippus, 50; *ill.*, 52-53

Insect, advanced, 17
  anatomy, 17
  ancestral tree, *ill.*, 110
  development, 17; *ill.*, 111
  disguises, 43, 35
  economic importance, 17
  instinct, 44, 95
  leaf, 45
  metamorphosis, 17; *ill.*, 111
  "mimics," 44, 46, 61; *ill.*, 46, 47
  "models," 44, 46, 60, 86; *ill.*, 46, 47
  predators, 83, 84
  protected, 45
  warning colors, 48
Interference, *see* Light
Iridescence, 22
Ithomiids, 37, 49
Ituna, 37
Larva, 17
  butterfly, *see* Caterpillar
  definition, 115
Leaf insect, 45
Lepidoptera, definition, 16
Light and color (*see also* Color)
  diffusion, 22
  interference, 22
  refraction, 21
Lycorea, 37

Mantids, 83, 84 (*see also* Praying Mantis)
Melanin, 21
Membrane, 19
Metamorphosis, definition, 17, 115
  complex, *ill.*, 111
  gradual, *ill.*, 111
Migration, 89-100
  bird, 89, 93
  butterfly, 90; *ill.*, 91
  monarch, 90-100; *ill.*, 88-89, 98-99
Milkweed, 23, 28, 65, 103, 104; *ill.*, 105
  (*see also* Asclepias plants toxicity, 28, 29)
Milkweed butterflies, 23, 24, 28
  (*see also* Danaids; Monarch)

Index

African, 33, 34; *ill.*, 30-31
caterpillars, 24; *ill.*, 33, 64-65, 67, 69, 74, 75
Central American, 36, 37, 40; *ill.*, 38-39
colors, 23
distastefulness, 29
food plants, 23
habits, 24
immunity, 46-47, 50
Indo-Australian, 35; *ill.*, 30-31, 35
"mimics," 49, 61; *ill.*, 42-43
"models," 49, 60, 86; *ill.*, 42-43, 48
North American, 57-62,
 (*see also* Monarch; Queen)
poison, 29
protection, 33
South American, 36-37, 40, 54; *ill.*, 38-39
warning colors, 32
"Mimic" (*see also* Insect, "mimics")
 beetle, 46
 butterfly, 49-51; *ill.*, 42-43, 48
 grasshopper, 46
 moth, 46; *ill.*, 46, 47
Mimicry, definition, 44, 115; 43-54
 advantages, 54
 Batesian, 49, 51
 Müllerian, 51, 54
"Model," definition, 115 (*see also* Insect, "models")
 beetle, *ill.*, 47
 bumblebee, 45, 46
 hornet, 45-47, *ill.*, 46
 wasp, 46
Molt, 68, 70
 definition, 116
Monarch, 23, 57-62, 76-78, 81-86, 90-97, 103-107; *ill.*, 57, 77, 81, 83, 85, 88-89, 95, 103, 107
 African, 33, 34, 50, 51; *ill.*, 30, 52
 behavior, 58
 caterpillar, 65-70; *ill.*, 64-65, 67, 69, 74-75
 chrysalis, 73-78; *ill.*, 72-73, 76, 103

colors, 58, 77, 82
distastefulness, 58
distribution, 61; *ill.*, 59
egg, 65-66; *ill.* 66
food plant, 65, 70
habits, 62
instinct, 95
life span, 85
metamorphosis, 70
migration, 90-97; *ill.*, 88-89, 91-92, 98-99
North American, 23, 57-62, 76-78, 90-97, 103-107
pattern, 58
protection, 58
raising, 103-107
sense of taste, 19
Morphoes, 22, 28; *ill.*, 20, 21
Moths, 16, 17; *ill.*, 18
 economic importance, 17
 "mimics," *ill.*, 46, 47
Müller, Fritz, 51, 54

Natural selection theory, 46, 47
Nymphalid, 50
 "mimic," *ill.*, 49

Order, definition of zoological term, 116

Pacific Grove, 96
Painted lady, 90; *ill.*, 91
 (*see also* Thistle butterfly)
Papilio dardanus, 50, 51; *ill.* 52-53
Patterns of butterfly wings, 19; *ill.*, 20, 22
 camouflage, 44
 warning, 32, 45, 48
Pierinae, 49 (*see also* Whites)
Pigments, 20, 21
Praying mantis, 83, 84; *ill.*, 82
Proboscis, 18; *ill.*, 112 (*see also* Sucking tube)
 definition, 116
Proleg, 68; *ill.* 113
 definition, 116

119

Index

Protected, definition of zoological term, 116
Pupa, 17 *(see also* Chrysalis)
   definition 73, 116

Queen, 61, 62; *ill.,* 61

Scales, *see* Butterfly, scales
Silkworm, 69
Skipper, *ill.,* 18
Species, definition of zoological term, 116
Spinneret, 69; *ill.,* 113
   definition, 116
Spiracle, 19; *ill.,* 112, 113
   definition, 116
Stick insect, 45; *ill.,* 44
Structural colors, *see* Colors, structural
Sucking tube, 18 *(see also* Proboscis)

Survival of the fittest, 47 *(see also* Natural selection)
Swallowtail, 50; *ill.,* 18
   African, 51; *ill.,* 52-53
   Giant, 58

Thistle butterfly, *see* Painted Lady
Thorax, 17; *ill.,* 112, 113
   definition, 116
"Tiger," 35 *(see also* Danaus chrysippus)
Tongue of butterfly, *see* Proboscis
Trachea, definition, 116

Viceroy, 61; *ill.,* 60

Wallace, Alfred R., 47, 51
Whites, 49 *(see also* Cabbage butterfly; Pierinae)

3 9123 00154786 3
HACKENSACK-JOHNSON LIBRARY
a3912300154786 3b

DATE DUE

J595.7   232775
Simon
Milkweed butterflies.

~~781~~
633

Johnson Free Public Library
Hackensack, New Jersey